Exmouth

IEMATICS

UITY IN MATHEMATICS
; WITHIN LEVEL 1

NES

A NASEN Publication

Published in 1999

ISBN 1 901485 06 4

Published by NASEN.
NASEN is a registered charity. Charity No. 1007023.
NASEN is a company limited by guarantee, registered in England and Wales.
Company No. 2674379.

Further copies of this book and details of NASEN's many other publications may be obtained from the NASEN Bookshop at its registered office:
NASEN House, 4/5, Amber Business Village, Amber Close, Amington, Tamworth, Staffs., B77 4RP.
Tel: 01827 311500  Fax: 01827 313005 email: welcome@nasen.org.uk
Website: www.nasen.org.uk

Cover design by Raphael Creative Design.
Typeset by J. C. Typesetting.
Typeset in Times and printed in the United Kingdom by Stowes (Stoke-on-Trent).

# SPIRAL MATHEMATICS

## Contents

# SPIRAL MATHEMATICS
## Progression and Continuity in Mathematics for Pupils Working within Level 1

## Acknowledgements

My thanks to staff at Meldreth Manor School for their contributions and comments throughout the development of this work. In particular the work completed by Liz Grey and Hazel Cant when they were mathematics co-ordinators at the school. In addition the thoughts and contributions of Myles Pilling when this work was in earlier incarnations cannot be overemphasised.

# Chapter 1 - What is Mathematics?

## Introduction

Is mathematics important? Is there any reason why so much time should be spent looking at the curriculum offered to pupils with severe or profound learning difficulties and seeking to enhance, broaden and extend that curriculum by implementing the skills and understandings described in the National Curriculum Programmes of Study for Mathematics and those within the National Numeracy Strategy? I cannot answer these questions as a mathematician, since my own skills in mathematics are rudimentary. I could never crack Rubik's cube and my local authority refused to let me add up my own travel claims as the answers were never the same twice. But I can answer as a teacher of pupils with special needs, and most especially of those with profound learning difficulties. Mathematics is important to these pupils because it provides a way of viewing and understanding the world in which we live. All pupils, regardless of their abilities, need to be offered a range of ways to explore the world in which they find themselves. All pupils need to explore and understand the world through their physical senses. They need to appreciate artistic and creative ways of describing that world, but they also need to develop those skills that are defined as mathematical. These are concerned with looking at the world in a logical manner, and provide the means to describe much else that we learn. Mathematics is a key component of developing real independence for children with learning difficulties. Independence can be seen as having three components:

- *Communication* - asking questions, giving instructions, interacting with the world through language. For pupils with profound and multiple learning difficulties (PMLD) this may mean developing a yes/no response, communicating meaning through gesture or through symbols.
- *Mobility* - the physical skills by which we can manipulate the world around us, and manoeuvre ourselves through that world. For pupils with PMLD this may mean developing the control over our body to maintain position and point clearly to objects or symbols.
- *Cognition* - the ability to make sense of the world around us, through an understanding of the complex relationships and interactions between parts of that world. Again, for pupils with PMLD this may be concerned with an understanding of the cause and effect or anticipating events.

Mathematics is about assimilating information, understanding it and making decisions based upon that understanding. Without these skills we remain dependent upon the skills and knowledge of others. If we wish to promote independence amongst all our children we must then include mathematics in their curriculum.

## Defining the subject

Mathematics is threatening. In the opening to this book I made light of my inability to add a simple column of figures. When asked to recall mathematics at school, many teachers whom I have worked with cast their minds back to tests and exams. They often describe emotions including panic, fear, worry, embarrassment and so on. This immense sense of unease that many teachers face when asked to explore mathematics has been described as 'maths panic' (Burton, 1981).

*The Maths Bomb*

For many, mathematics has been seen as a set of arbitrary rules that are difficult to master and accessible to the few. One of the challenges that faces us is to define mathematics as the study of relationships accessible to all, but which can be explored in greater or lesser depth by individuals.

In beginning to plan for the delivery of a broad, balanced and relevant mathematics curriculum in schools for pupils with PMLD we must discard some of our own emotional baggage and look again at the nature of mathematics. Earlier I gave some simple definitions; these build upon those suggested by the National Curriculum Council in 1991. More recently definitions of mathematics have been offered within the 1999 revised National Curriculum and the National Numeracy Strategy - 1999.

*'Mathematics contributes to the school curriculum by developing pupils' abilities to calculate, to reason logically ... to solve problems and to handle data ... It is also important in everyday living, in many forms of employment and in public decision making ... mathematics presents frequent opportunities for creativity and can stimulate moments of pleasure and wonder when a problem is solved for the first time ...*

*... the power of mathematical reasoning lies in its use of precise and concise forms of language, symbolism and representation to reveal and explore general relationships.'* (DfEE/QCA, 1999)

Within the National Numeracy Strategy further clarity is offered in defining numeracy:

*'Numeracy is a proficiency which involves confidence and competence with numbers and measures. It requires an understanding of the number system, a repertoire of computational skills and an inclination and an ability to solve number problems in a variety of contexts.'*
(DfEE, 1999, p4)

In addition there is a need to have an understanding of each of the areas of mathematics before we can seek to implement them with pupils of whatever ability.

The National Curriculum for Mathematics is divided into four attainment targets and related programmes of study for each of the four key stages. Running throughout each of these attainment targets are a number of mathematical strands.

The four attainment targets are:

|  | KS1 | KS2 | KS3 | KS4 |
|---|---|---|---|---|
| AT1 | Using and Handling | Using and Handling | Using and Handling | Using and Handling |
| AT2 | Number | Number | Number and Algebra | Number and Algebra |
| AT3 | Shape Space and Measures | Shape Space and Measures | Shape Space and Measures | Shape Space and Measures |
| AT4 |  | Handling Data | Handling Data | Handling Data |

## Using and Handling

The first of these describes the mathematical process, and the skills and understanding that pupils need to develop to make use of the skills which are being developed in each of the other attainment target areas. Thus, this attainment target permeates and integrates the other areas of mathematics.

## Number

The second area is that of number. Number provides the language and the symbols by which we can communicate in shorthand our understanding of the relationships between objects in the world around us. The skills, which together make up an ability to use number, are in themselves complex and demand a high level of cognitive ability from pupils. Merely to count demands from pupils an ability to complete a range of tasks:

- to recall number names;
- to allocate those names one to each member of a group;
- to remember which items in a set have already been given a number;
- to understand that the number allocated to the last object in the group is also the number given to the whole group.

Numbers are far from easy to work with. A structured approach to understanding the complexity of number has been provided by Roy McConkey in the *Count Me In* video course available from St Michael's House School in Ireland.

## Algebra

At KS3 and 4 algebra is introduced into the curriculum alongside number. The very name seems to instil concerns into teachers. Yet it is much more straightforward than at first is apparent. At the early stage of development, algebra is concerned with the identification and understanding of pattern, and of the relationships that create patterns. These patterns can be in time, in colour or in any physical characteristic. The use of the shorthand that we are all familiar with as 'algebraic equations etc.' is simply one way of describing a pattern.

**Shape, space and measurement**

The third area of mathematics is that of shape, space and measurement, and is, of course, much more teacher-friendly, in name if not content, than that of algebra. Shape and space is concerned with an understanding of the properties of shapes in the world, and begins with the relationship between our own bodies and the physical world, an understanding of our position relative to space. For many pupils the ability to explore shapes and sizes may provide a great degree of access to mathematics, and in seeking to find ways to describe their understanding of how shapes and objects compare, pupils begin to use skills related to algebra and number.

---

**Example - Human turtles**

A group of pupils are working in the school hall. On a flip chart are large rebus symbols for left, right, forward and reverse. Pupils in powered chairs or with assistants are acting out the part of turtles following the directions and instructions of the turtle master guiding them from A to B to find treasure.

---

**Handling data**

The final area of the mathematics curriculum is that of handling data. This area of the curriculum is concerned with gathering information from the world around us and identifying ideas based upon that information. There is included in such a process the earliest stages of probability, the constant questioning 'what will happen now?' Prediction can occur in any of the areas of mathematics but is specifically related here to identifying ideas, and representing that information in a way that is understandable by others.

---

**Example - What will happen next?**

A group of pupils are baking a cake. A game is played out where the pupils must guess what will happen to another cake if the teacher increases the temperature of the oven from gas mark 6 to gas mark 8. A third cake is then baked and the pupils must guess what it will be like when it comes out after baking at gas mark 2 for the same amount of time.

---

**Progression in the mathematical strands**

Each of the strands we have discussed above follow a broadly hierarchical nature and reflect the levels of the National Curriculum. The National Curriculum structure is based upon a more focused and narrower range of content at the early key stages. This principle, that at the earliest levels of mathematics the content of the curriculum may be more focused or less broad than at higher levels, is one which I will apply more broadly in approaching the curriculum for pupils within level 1.

In addition we can recognise that the development of mathematical understanding in one strand draws upon the development of skills from other themes. It is not until these skills have been thoroughly learnt and attainment demonstrated that we then move on to use those skills in new ways, in other areas. This interrelationship is complex; and it lies at the heart of the principle of a spiral model of progression. In addition, these strands of mathematical activity are particularly useful when we look later at differentiating an activity, that is the development of activities through which pupils of differing abilities are learning related skills in a single group setting.

It is these twin notions of skills being learnt at an appropriate level coupled with the interrelationship of the differing elements of the curriculum that will be returned to later.

These areas of mathematics taken from the National Curriculum differ slightly from those within the National Numeracy Strategy by identifying five strands:

- Numbers and the number system
- Calculations
- Solving problems
- Measures, shape and space
- Handling data

Within the National Numeracy Strategy documentation, reference is made to the application of the framework within special schools. Whilst the underlying principle of inclusivity should be applauded, the advice is somewhat scant and unhelpful.

'... It is possible that in some special schools all or nearly all of the pupils in a class have learning difficulties that extend to mathematics. In this case it may be best to base the work for Key Stages 1 and 2 on the teaching programmes for reception and Years 1 and 2. Taking two years to cover what will be taught in one year in mainstream. Extra small steps can be inserted, and contexts for practical work and problem solving adapted for the pupils' ages. There will then be plenty of time for consolidation without sacrificing the breadth of teaching programmes...'                                                                     (DfEE, 1999, p24)

This guidance appears to completely ignore the needs of pupils who are likely to work within level 1 for most if not all of their school careers.

The development of the application of the strategy for pupils with such complex needs can sensibly make use of some of the principles of the strategy - a focus upon mathematics each day, clear objectives, links between home and school etc. There is, however, a need for a structure which will facilitate very early mathematical learning.

Within *Spiral Mathematics* I will make reference both to a range of activities and to early mathematical outcomes to help schools address this shortfall.

## Entering the National Curriculum - Government initiatives

Over the past three years the Government agencies have offered two significant initiatives in helping map the curriculum for children working before level 1.

The 'desirable outcomes' describe the achievements that a child is expected to have made before beginning compulsory schooling through attending nursery schools, and the 'P-levels' describing routes of progress for children working within level 1 of the National Curriculum to inform target setting in schools (SCAA, 1996; DfEE, 1998).

## Desirable outcomes - Early Years Curriculum

The material contained within the *Desirable Outcomes for Children's Learning on Entering Compulsory Schooling* (SCAA, 1996) offers brief descriptions of the stage of development a child should have reached upon entering compulsory schooling. In preparing the materials for this book, I have attempted to ensure that the extended programmes of study are relevant to the structure of this phase of education as well as the compulsory years. The ethos throughout the extended programmes of study is entirely in keeping with that of SCAA (now QCA in 1998) in that:

'They focus on achievement through practical activities and on using and understanding language in the development of simple mathematical ideas.'                     (SCAA, 1996, p3)

The desirable outcomes expressed for mathematics are succinct:

'Children use mathematical language such as circle, in front of, bigger than and more to describe shape, position, size and quantity. They recognise and recreate patterns. They begin to use their developing mathematical understanding to solve practical problems.' (p3)

'They are familiar with number rhymes, songs, stories, counting games and activities. They compare, match, order, sequence and count using everyday objects. They recognise and use numbers to 10 and are familiar with larger numbers from their everyday lives. Through practical activities children understand and record numbers, begin to show awareness of number operations, such as addition and subtraction, and begin to use the language involved.' (p3)

Whilst recognising that these outcomes are the subject of further review, the schemes of work and steps in the Spiral Mathematics curriculum are one way in which young children, both chronologically and developmentally, can progress towards their achievement.

## The development of the P-levels

*Supporting the target setting process*, DfEE (1998) sought to offer schools guidance on charting the progress of children working within levels 1 and 2 of the National Curriculum. This guidance was principally to provide a system by which schools could provide performance data about themselves.

Within the P-levels there are three scales, in language and literacy, personal and social development and mathematics. Each of these has eight descriptions leading to level 1 of the National Curriculum, and three differentiated descriptions within each of level 1 and level 2 of the National Curriculum. For mathematics, scales are offered for Number, Using and Applying and Shape, Space and Measures.

The structure of the eight P-levels is of relevance to this work in that from P1-P8 the outcomes are not only common across all three of the scales for mathematics but also across all of the scales in the other areas. The scales then differentiate into different mathematical strands from P4-P8. Within the work on the spiral model there is an understanding that there are a tightly entwined set of skills relating to the development of interactive skills that encompass all areas of early development. However, the materials differ from those within the P-scales in that there is an attempt to differentiate the strands of mathematics from other areas to help teachers set meaningful targets for pupils at the earliest stages of development.

# Chapter 2 - The Spiral Mathematics Model

Much has been said in recent years about how we should seek to move away from the categorisation of special educational needs by labels and towards a model in which all pupils are defined as having individual needs. Accepting this premise, the pupils for whom this model of curriculum is appropriate are amongst those whose individual needs are most complex. The pupils we are seeking to develop make up a tiny minority of the population of schools, and are functioning at the earliest levels of any form of cognitive scale that one might wish to use. They may, however, have a breadth of experience of activities, events and people which they can draw upon in the classroom.

## Pupils with learning difficulties and mathematical learning

The curriculum for children with severe or profound and multiple learning difficulties has been the subject of much speculation over the past 10 years. In evolving a model that is effective there have been many influences. There are many stakeholders in this process: teachers, therapists, assistants, parents, the pupils themselves etc. Whereas in English, teachers have a rich heritage of the development of language and communication in children with PMLD to draw upon, despite such innovations as the Montessori approach, no such diverse history exists for mathematics.

There are a number of reviews of the models of special education that have contributed to the current position. One which is useful to refer to is that within Rose, Sebba and Byers (1993).

## The curriculum for pupils with profound and multiple learning difficulties

Carol Ouvry (1990) has divided the curriculum for pupils with PMLD into three overlapping areas. These areas are National Curriculum, Developmental Curriculum and therapeutic approaches.

These have been most successfully represented in diagrammatic form.

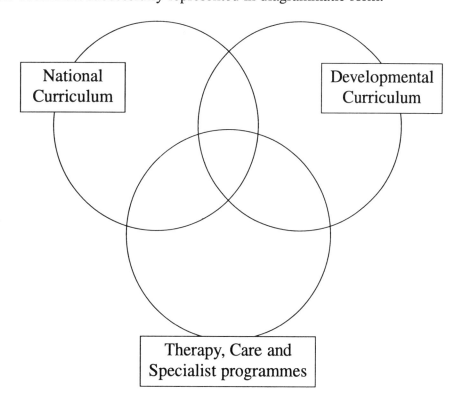

We can look at these distinctions more clearly when related to the development of language. We can distinguish between the programmes of study for English - speaking and listening, reading and writing etc, providing a range of contexts in which language and communication are taught and a hierarchy of skills and knowledge as outcomes within those contexts. A developmental approach of 'communication', focusing upon the stages of development that a child goes through from birth to competency, and incorporating verbal and non-verbal approaches, and the role of speech and language therapy in providing a language focus in which linguistic structures can be analysed and further developed.

These three strands interplay in creating structures for assessment and offer both diverse contexts within which learning can be ensured and offer teachers the opportunity to tailor a programme to individual needs.

In exploring mathematics there are two strands which overlap in creating the curriculum: the National Curriculum for mathematics, as described in Chapter 1, and the developmental approach which can be referred to as 'Numeracy', which describes the route which pupils take in developing the skills that are defined within the more traditional National Curriculum.

Whilst mathematics as a discrete subject can be drawn from the National Curriculum, it is learnt in activities that can be planned through any or all of the above. Additionally, Numeracy across the curriculum can provide a framework in which mathematical skills are developed, whilst the therapeutic approach to the use of these skills may fall within the domain of psychologists.

Such distinctions are mostly meaningless to the daily experience of the child. Any or all of the interrelated perspectives will be brought to bear through a series of object and social interactions. In *Curriculum Guidance 9* (NCC, 1991), the National Curriculum Council identified these two types of activity, which contribute to the curriculum for pupils with SLD/PMLD.

In developing the materials discussed here, I have attempted to extend this distinction and classification of activities, and to integrate these into the planning of activities for pupils so as to ensure that the experiences are relevant to both age and ability. In analysing the mathematics curriculum with teachers, great care has been taken to ensure that any model offered is linked to clearly stated pupil needs.

The activities discussed at the earliest stages of development are designed to promote the interactions discussed above. They are about learning to relate to people, both adults and peers, and about exploring and establishing control over objects within the personal environment.

It is in establishing an understanding of these relationships with people and objects that pupils are developing fundamental mathematical skills, enmeshed in a cross-curricular network of learning. As these skills develop they may develop in differing areas of the curriculum, in communication, in social learning and also in mathematics.

Ultimately the curriculum for all pupils must be broad, balanced and relevant. The mathematics curriculum described here is a part of just such a curriculum.

## Spiral Mathematics

The curriculum developed for pupils with learning difficulties must provide for appropriate access to all, and then should identify pathways of progression for pupils. The notion of the spiral curriculum is based upon the idea that there are a variety of forms of progression that can built into the curriculum of pupils with SLD/PMLD.

### 1) Vertical Progression

This is the traditional form of progression and is the closest to the form exemplified in the National Curriculum itself.

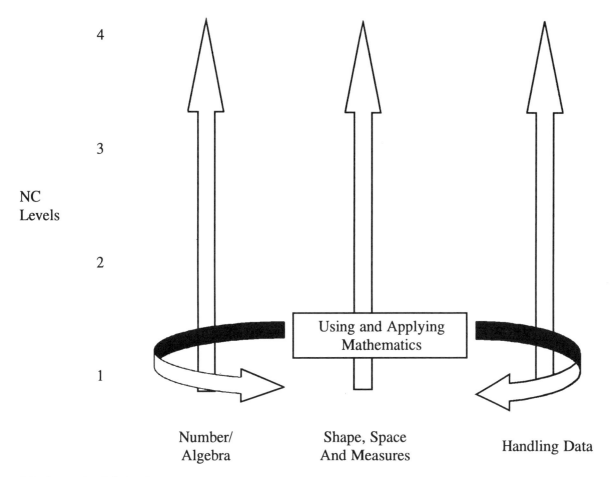

4

3

NC
Levels

2

Using and Applying
Mathematics

1

Number/
Algebra

Shape, Space
And Measures

Handling Data

*Mathematical Strands*

It can be likened to that of a ladder which leads upwards through a number of targets. It was first well demonstrated for this group of pupils in the Manchester Teacher Fellows materials *Maths for All* (1993). In this the MEC teacher fellows have looked specifically at AT1 'Using and Applying Mathematics' and have created a number of milestones leading to attainment and a curriculum at level 1.

More recently, valuable work was completed by 'Equals' in developing the 'Access' materials. Within this model a more complex structure is proposed making distinct the key strands of the mathematical curriculum. The areas in which they identify programmes of study are:

• **Early Concepts**

The pupil shows development from simple reflexive responses to stimuli to a growing understanding of the world. They come to view themselves as active agents in the learning process by experiencing situations where their interactions with objects and people result in rewarding reactions. Early cognitive development takes place when the child is offered stimulating, rewarding experiences that allow them to use and further develop their existing concepts.

• **Using and Applying Maths**

The pupil will demonstrate an understanding of the classification of objects and group objects according to shape, size, colour and quantity by his/her ability to carry out tasks. The pupil shows familiarity with number and the development of the ability to compare, sort, match, order, sequence and count. He/she is developing early number operations and mathematical language as well as recognising and recreating patterns.

- **Familiarity with Number**

The development of the ability to compose, sort, match, order, sequence and count. The development of early number operations and an introduction to mathematical language.

- **Recognising and Recreating Patterns**

The recognition of patterns around us and the knowledge that they can be continued (Equals, 1997, p1).

Within their work they also make useful reference to a key principle that informs the spiral model:

> *'Although the programmes of study for mathematics are generally hierarchical, it will be necessary from time to time to revisit previous programmes in order to facilitate further progress.'*
> (Equals, 1997, p8)

The development of preliminary statements of attainment to level 1, and a graded programme of study within level 1, offer much to anyone wishing to develop a curriculum for pupils with SLD/PMLD. In this case, however, whilst I wish to incorporate these ideas, I also wish to offer a model of curriculum which indicates the interrelationship between the attainment targets.

### 2) Horizontal Progression

This form of progression takes two forms. First, that of students practising and generalising their skills in an increasingly wide variety of contexts, which broadens the scope in which that skill is demonstrated.

The second form is based in the relationship between the areas of mathematics described in the National Curriculum strands, and is concerned with the ways in which skills developed in one area, will provide the foundations of skills which lie within another strand.

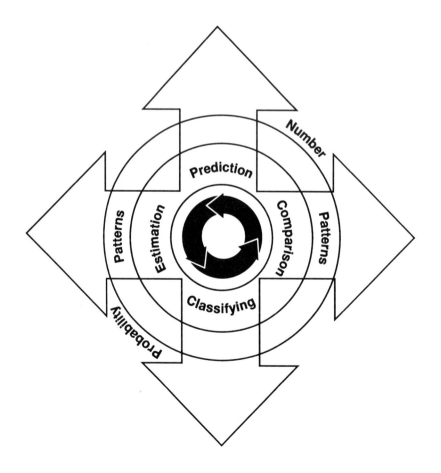

The diagram seeks to suggest that there are three phases of development within level 1. At Phase 1 early development addresses estimation, classification, comparison and prediction. At Phase 2 development in these aspects continues and children draw these together to begin to recognise and relate to pattern. At Phase 3 the child's understanding of pattern is such that they use symbols including numbers to represent the patterns and structures and are able to use their imagination to consider likelihood and probability.

The arrows suggest that as these aspects become integrated there is still scope for children to continue to develop with one of the aspects from an earlier stage of development. Hence development in making mathematical comparison occurs at all three phases.

In this model, there are a limited number of skills, which provide a core for future development. For example, a child develops skills in an area such as prediction. These are vertically developed as the child is able to make more expansive predictions from less concrete information, and in addition the child uses his/her skills to provide the foundation for learning about pattern and a wider network of relationships.

In combining these two forms of progression I use the term 'Spiral Mathematics'. This describes a curriculum that starts from a narrow base of foundation skills, which then broadens through a range of contexts. In parallel there is a corresponding increase in the complexity of the skills being used which also provide the basis for new skills that can be further developed.

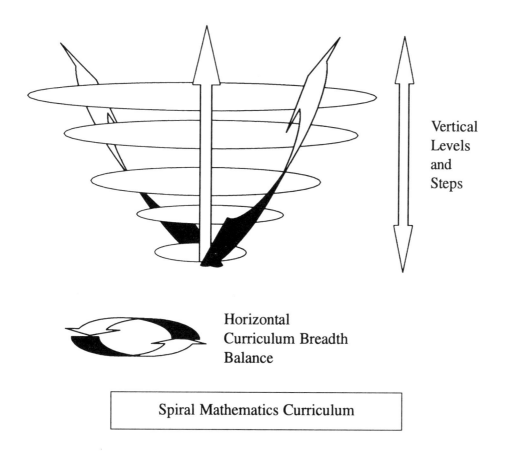

Vertical
Levels
and
Steps

Horizontal
Curriculum Breadth
Balance

Spiral Mathematics Curriculum

Having introduced this model of the curriculum, I now wish to look at these three broad phases of development within level 1 of the National Curriculum. Whilst these phases will ultimately lead to attainment at level 1 of the Mathematics National Curriculum, it would be wrong to see them as stepping stones towards that attainment. Rather they can be seen as a further development of the programmes of study at level 1. The activities and phases of development operate across all key stages. However, we shall return to the issue of key stage appropriateness at a later point in this discussion.

## Phase 1
### The introductory level

The curriculum for mathematics at this level is concerned with the development of three strands of mathematical learning. These are

- Prediction/Anticipation
- Classification
- Comparison

The development of these concepts is going to be related to an introduction to shape, space and measurement through the movement of one's body in space, moving purposefully in a given direction and rotating that body to view objects in the environment from a range of different perspectives. Equally, in making the earliest comparisons between objects, pupils will begin to appreciate quantity, one and more than one, more or less in a concrete way, working with materials that have meaning for the pupil such as food or drink.

## Phase 2
### The appreciation of pattern

As students develop the skills described above in phase 1, they begin to develop an understanding of the notion of pattern, as described in the programmes of study as an element of Number and Algebra. The curriculum for mathematics at this phase is thus concerned with:

- Patterns
- Prediction and Anticipation
- Classification
- Comparison
- Estimation

As students extend the skills described in phase 1 relating to comparisons of quantity, they must steadily begin to estimate quantities and sizes through exploration of objects and sets via their senses.

It is legitimate at this point to begin to talk about mathematical *activities* for pupils with severe or profound and multiple learning difficulties, as opposed to mathematical *elements* of cross-curricular activities.

## Phase 3
### The language level

The third phase of development in early mathematics is concerned with the discovery of a variety of ways of describing and communicating one's findings in mathematics. Activities might be related to making predictions about time and the pattern of the day or week. It is at this stage as well that pupils may begin to use number in a meaningful way to describe their discoveries. As pupils find a means to describe their predictions so they can begin to rationalise and consider the probability of likely events happening. Thus pupils can be introduced to concepts relating to AT5 'Handling Data'. At this stage it is fair to believe that pupils are working within the full range of the five attainment targets for mathematics in the National Curriculum.

Throughout this progression, access has been considered to be paramount. One of the most powerful tools available to teachers in accessing the full programmes of study for mathematics is that of information technology.

**Example - Pupils working with IT in mathematics**
Pupils are working with Writing with symbols (Widgit software) and Clicker (Crick Computing) to tally the people walking past their classroom by touching a symbol for male and a symbol for female. A second group of pupils have prepared a 10-person list predicting the number of men and women and the two groups will compare the results.

Having established the curriculum model to which the pupils are being taught, it is now appropriate to offer a broader range of examples of activities within each phase of development, and to consider the contexts within which these activities may be developed.

# Chapter 3 - Extended Programmes of Study for Mathematics

**Curriculum organisation**

The structure suggested here offers one means by which mathematical progression for all pupils can be planned and ensured. This offers the pupil a planned progression of mathematical content. We shall return later to planning for a progression throughout the mathematical strands to ensure an appropriate breadth of context.

In making use of the phases of development, the teacher should consider carefully the nature of social and object interactions that the child is encountering. Through observation of these events and the extended programmes offered below, the aspects of mathematical learning that are taking place can be identified. In using these programmes one can see that some aspects will progress vertically and others will be about developing additional skills within the same area. The teacher should seek to establish aims in both aspects of development.

| Phase | Strand | Level Description | Activities/Programmes of Study |
|---|---|---|---|
| 1. Introductory | Prediction/ Anticipation | **Early Development** P1 Pupils are beginning to show sensory awareness in relation to a range of people, objects and materials in everyday contexts. They show reflex responses to sensory stimuli. <br><br> P2 Pupils perform some actions using trial and error and show reactive responses to familiar people and objects. They make sounds or gestures to express simple needs, wants or feelings in response to their immediate environment. <br><br> P3 Pupils show anticipation in response to familiar people, routines, activities and actions and respond | 1) Pupils may initially make predictions through looking in a given direction for something to appear e.g. <br> • Looking towards the next lamp to be lit on a rope light strung across the classroom which is set to a sufficiently slow pace. <br> • Looking towards the other end of the tunnel in expectation of the train coming out when a toy train enters a tunnel strung across the floor. <br> • Tracking a ball on a length of chain which is swinging slowly behind a screen thus encouraging the pupil to look from one side to the other. <br><br> 2) Routines can be broken and staff can monitor pupils' responses e.g. <br> • Varying mealtimes by going on the minibus to a restaurant for lunch, rather than into the dining room. <br> • Varying and editing the tape of music which is used to introduce pupils to the classroom at 9.00. <br> • Serving the pupils their pudding before their savoury course and noting their responses. etc. |

| Phase | Strand | Level Description | Activities/Programmes of Study |
|---|---|---|---|
| | | appropriately to them. They explore or manipulate objects, toys or other equipment. They are able to communicate simple choices, likes and dislikes. They can communicate using different tones and sounds and use some vocalisations and/or gestures to communicate. | 3) Break patterns in activities and see if the pupils make any comment e.g.<br>• Singing hello to each pupil in turn during music, but then skipping one of the group and looking for any response.<br>• Asking pupils to place their hands in a feelie box to find a hidden object, periodically offering a pupil an empty bag.<br>• Giving a pupil a switch to operate the computer but without plugging it in and seeking a communication.<br>etc.<br><br>4) Staff can act in unexpected ways during an activity e.g.<br>• Acting as if one is going to break an egg into the toaster rather than into the frying pan.<br>• Dipping a knife into the paint rather than the jam to spread on bread.<br>• Instead of peeling an apple for a pupil hitting it with a hammer.<br>etc.<br><br>5) Staff can make use of a programmable toy such as a Roamer, Bigtrak or Pip where one press of the go button makes the toy take one movement forward.<br><br>Unexpected actions such as those described above can be gross or fine. This may well depend upon just how closely a routine is usually followed. If pupils are always offered a choice of biscuit at 11.00 simply not doing so may surprise the pupils on an occasion. Many of the activities can also progress by moving from the familiar to the less familiar, hence |

| Phase | Strand | Level Description | Activities/Programmes of Study |
|---|---|---|---|
| | | | cooking may be very familiar but the same variation whilst on a visit to the local museum may be less so. |
| 1. Introductory | Classification | **Early Development**<br>P1<br>Pupils are beginning to show sensory awareness in relation to a range of people, objects and materials in everyday contexts. They show reflex responses to sensory stimuli.<br><br>P2<br>Pupils perform some actions using trial and error and show reactive responses to familiar people and objects. They make sounds or gestures to express simple needs, wants or feelings in response to their immediate environment.<br><br>P3<br>Pupils show anticipation in response to familiar people, routines, activities and actions and respond appropriately to them. They explore or manipulate objects, toys or other equipment. They are able to communicate simple choices, likes and dislikes. They can communicate using different tones | 1) Pupils can explore a range of objects offered by a peer or member of staff and find an appropriate use for them e.g.<br>• Taking a cup and holding it up to the mouth.<br>• Taking a piece of string which hangs and pulling upon it.<br>• Finding a single switch upon the tray and pressing it.<br>• Holding an armband and looking towards the swimming pool door. etc.<br><br>2) Pupils can take objects that they find and use them in a manner which is logical, although not what they were designed for e.g.<br>• Finding a rattle and using it to make patterns in the sand tray.<br>• Using a paintbrush to tap out on a table top.<br>• Using lunch as a modelling material. etc.<br><br>3) Pupils attempt to use objects in a familiar way and then discover that some of the properties of the object have altered e.g.<br>• Exploring a squeezy bottle which was filled with beans, and recognising that change has occurred when it is filled with water and shaken.<br>• Discovering that a piece of tinsel, which was attached to several sets of bells, is now attached to several balloons.<br>• Finding that the sand tray is filled with ball pool balls rather than the usual sand. etc. |

| Phase | Strand | Level Description | Activities/Programmes of Study |
|---|---|---|---|
| | | and sounds and use some vocalisations and/or gestures to communicate. | 4) Pupils may communicate their awareness of a change in what they have expected to be the properties of a familiar object e.g.<br>• Crying out when the dinner plate turns out to be full of paint.<br>• Laughing when the switch on the tray operates a set of bells rather than a communication machine.<br>• Looking around for help when the squeezy bottle with a few lentils in is changed for a similar one that is full of sand and much heavier.<br>etc.<br><br>5) Pupils use a movement for a specific purpose e.g.<br>• Waving hands to communicate goodbye.<br>• Kicking legs to trip up a member of staff.<br>• Raising arms to pull on ribbons that are attached to another pupil.<br>• Lifting one's head to activate a pressure pad that works the computer.<br>etc.<br><br>6) Pupils sort through a range of play materials for a particular reason e.g.<br>• Discarding all the contents of a box in search of a favoured soft toy.<br>• Rejecting a switch because the pupil doesn't like the computer it used to be attached to.<br>• Picking a grip switch out of a selection of odds and ends because that was attached to the Pethna.<br>• Choosing only the wheeled objects out of a set in a box because the pupil likes to roll them off the edge of his wheelchair tray.<br>etc. |

| Phase | Strand | Level Description | Activities/Programmes of Study |
|---|---|---|---|
| 1. Introductory | Comparison | **Early Development**<br>P1<br>Pupils are beginning to show sensory awareness in relation to a range of people, objects and materials in everyday contexts. They show reflex responses to sensory stimuli.<br><br>P2<br>Pupils perform some actions using trial and error and show reactive responses to familiar people and objects. They make sounds or gestures to express simple needs, wants or feelings in response to their immediate environment.<br><br>P3<br>Pupils show anticipation in response to familiar people, routines, activities and actions and respond appropriately to them. They explore or manipulate objects, toys or other equipment. They are able to communicate simple choices, likes and dislikes. They can communicate using different tones and sounds and use some vocalisations and/or gestures to communicate. | Comparison<br>1) A pupil may examine two objects and choose which of them to keep e.g.<br>• Taking a cake rather than a biscuit from the offered tray.<br>• Choosing the James Brown rather than the Mozart tape.<br>• Selecting paints rather than clay for the art lesson.<br>• Choosing the blue material rather than the red for the new curtains.<br>etc.<br><br>2) Pupils may be helped to sort through a collection of objects to find those they prefer e.g.<br>• Finding objects that rattle.<br>• Finding objects that are soft.<br>• Finding objects that flash.<br>etc.<br><br>3) When a pupil communicates a need such as 'I'm hungry' offer the pupil a choice between an object that meets that need and another which may be of another interest e.g.<br>• After stating that he/she is hungry a pupil might choose between a toy train and a packet of crisps.<br>• Offering pupils the choice between being picked up or watching a favourite video after a communication.<br>• When a pupil is building with one colour bricks and runs out, offering a choice between the same colour and one that is different.<br>etc.<br><br>4) Pupils can be offered comparisons in a wider range of settings e.g.<br>• Being pushed quickly or slowly in a wheelchair. |

| Phase | Strand | Level Description | Activities/Programmes of Study |
|---|---|---|---|
| | | | • Being out in the rain or under an umbrella. |
| | | | • Standing in a frame or lying across a roll. etc. |
| | | | 5) Breaking the pattern of expectation of the pupil can encourage comparison skills e.g. |
| | | | • Putting a green glove on one hand and then a red mitten on the other. |
| | | | • Dividing the lunch between two trolleys and asking pupils to examine the contents of each. |
| | | | • Choosing which of their physiotherapy exercises they want to do next rather than simply following the routine. etc. |
| | | | The above communications to indicate preferences can be assessed and formalised by careful use of a communication assessment tool such as the Affective Communication Assessment (see Coupe and Goldbart, 1988). |
| | | | 6) Use control technology to encourage pupils to compare the results of actions they are making e.g. |
| | | | • Using a simple electronic communicator programmed with two differing messages attached to two individual switches. |
| | | | • Using two switches which are connected via mains control boxes to two completely different pieces of equipment, such as a tape player and a rope light. |
| | | | • Using two switches on a computer to make an animated figure perform different actions. etc. |

| Phase | Strand | Level Description | Activities/Programmes of Study |
|---|---|---|---|
| | | | 7) The use of simple rebus symbols to facilitate choice and decision making must involve simple comparison skills e.g. <br> • Choosing between the symbol for cake and biscuit. <br> • Choosing between rebuses for swim and chair to describe an activity. <br> • Using a switch on the computer to highlight a particular symbol. |
| Phase 1 - The Introductory Level | Estimation | **Early Development** <br> P1 <br> Pupils are beginning to show sensory awareness in relation to a range of people, objects and materials in everyday contexts. They show reflex responses to sensory stimuli. <br><br> P2 <br> Pupils perform some actions using trial and error and show reactive responses to familiar people and objects. They make sounds or gestures to express simple needs, wants or feelings in response to their immediate environment. <br><br> P3 <br> Pupils show anticipation in response to familiar people, routines, activities and actions and respond appropriately to them. They explore | At this early level, estimation is very much related to body awareness and the relationship between body and the environment. There is also a close relationship with the strand of prediction. <br> 1) Pupils should be given opportunities to time responses through estimating when a desired object is within reach e.g. <br> • Holding a teddy bear above the child's head, encouraging them to reach and touch. <br> • Playing tickle games where the child is awaiting the hand to touch them. <br> • Bringing the adult's face closer to the child to encourage reaching and touching. <br><br> 2) The child should have opportunities to play with materials that will fill/overfill containers e.g. <br> • Playing with water and cups etc. <br> • Playing with sand and other discontinuous materials. <br><br> 3) The child should have opportunities to manoeuvre him or herself into positions which offer access to desired objects and people e.g. <br> • Using a powered wheelchair track to 'run over' a member of staff and laughing as they draw closer. |

| Phase | Strand | Level Description | Activities/Programmes of Study |
|---|---|---|---|
| | | or manipulate objects, toys or other equipment. They are able to communicate simple choices, likes and dislikes. They can communicate using different tones and sounds and use some vocalisations and/or gestures to communicate.<br><br>**Shape, Space and Measures**<br>P4<br>Pupils react to and begin to search for objects that have gone out of sight, hearing or touch. They begin to understand position and the relationship between objects, such as stacking or aligning objects. | • Using a walking aid to 'nudge' a football.<br>   etc.<br><br>4) The pupils will use an object such as a stick or stool to help when an object is out of reach e.g.<br>• Using a stick to push over a tower of bricks.<br>• Using a stool to reach a table top to get a biscuit.<br>• Rolling a ball to knock down objects when they can't be reached such as in skittles. |
| 2. The appreciation of pattern | Prediction | **Early Development**<br>P3<br>Pupils show anticipation in response to familiar people, routines, activities and actions and respond appropriately to them. They explore or manipulate objects, toys or other equipment. They are able to communicate simple choices, likes and dislikes. They can communicate using different tones and sounds and use | At this level the recognition of pattern and anticipation and prediction are going to be closely related.<br>1) Pupils should be predicting a number of steps in a sequence e.g.<br>• That a sequence of actions makes the computer work, put in the disc, click the mouse, move the pointer etc.<br>• That if you have beans, bread and butter in your trolley there are a number of actions that you need to make to cook beans on toast.<br>• That the third shape in a sequence will be a square.<br>   etc. |

| Phase | Strand | Level Description | Activities/Programmes of Study |
|-------|--------|-------------------|-------------------------------|
| | | some vocalisations and/or gestures to communicate.<br><br>**Using and Applying**<br>P4<br>Pupils demonstrate an awareness of cause and effect for familiar objects and activities.<br><br>P5<br>Pupils match with help objects and/or pictures. They group or sort sets of objects by characteristics such as size or shape.<br><br>P6<br>Pupils copy simple patterns or sequences. They sort objects but do not always consistently apply the criterion chosen.<br><br>**Shape, Space and Measures**<br>P4<br>Pupils react to and begin to search for objects that have gone out of sight, hearing or touch. They begin to understand position and the relationship between objects, such as stacking or aligning objects.<br><br>P5<br>Pupils react to and begin to search for objects that are in | 2) Pupils should anticipate what will happen if you don't complete a task in a given manner e.g.<br>• If you don't turn off the grill the bread will burn.<br>• If I use paint to stick together a model it will fall apart.<br>• If you don't put ice into the freezer it will melt.<br>etc.<br><br>3) Pupils should also anticipate the outcomes of combinations of actions or materials e.g.<br>• If I mix blue, yellow and white paint together I will get?<br>• If I walk down the corridor and turn left and then walk to the end I will be outside... where?<br>• If I try to pick up the brick with an elastic band, the band will break.<br>etc.<br><br>4) A pupil might make predictions as to how an object might change after given actions e.g.<br>• If I put a crisp packet in the oven it will shrink.<br>• If I stretch a jumper the arms will be longer.<br>• If I put bread under the grill it will turn brown.<br>etc. |

| Phase | Strand | Level Description | Activities/Programmes of Study |
|---|---|---|---|
| | | their usual place. They manipulate positions.<br><br>P6<br>Pupils search for objects not found in their usual location. | |
| 2. The appreciation of pattern | Classification | **Early Development**<br>P3<br>Pupils show anticipation in response to familiar people, routines, activities and actions and respond appropriately to them. They explore or manipulate objects, toys or other equipment. They are able to communicate simple choices, likes and dislikes. They can communicate using different tones and sounds and use some vocalisations and/or gestures to communicate.<br><br>**Using and Applying**<br>P5<br>Pupils match with help objects and/or pictures. They group or sort sets of objects by characteristics such as size or shape.<br><br>P6<br>Pupils copy simple patterns or sequences. They sort objects but do not | 1) Pupils take similar objects and sort them into quite distinct groups e.g.<br>• Taking the cutlery and sorting it into knives, forks and spoons.<br>• Taking a box of bricks and sorting them into Stickle, Lego and foam bricks.<br>• Taking all the toy animals and sorting them into zoo and farm animals.<br>etc.<br><br>2) Pupils should be extending the range of criteria by which they classify objects, to include weight, height, magnetic etc.<br>• Asking pupils to sort through a range of tins to see which are attracted to a magnet.<br>• Asking pupils to look at themselves and decide who are the tallest three pupils in the class.<br>• Asking pupils to sort through pictures of transport to choose those which fly.<br>etc.<br><br>3) Pupils should also begin to classify objects and pictures according to more than one significant feature e.g.<br>• Choosing all the big chocolate biscuits from a tin.<br>• Picking all the tall round jars for pickling.<br>• Cutting the pastry with a small star-shaped pastry cutter. |

| Phase | Strand | Level Description | Activities/Programmes of Study |
|---|---|---|---|
| | | always consistently apply the criterion chosen. | • Finding all the red T-shirts for a team on sports day. etc. |
| | | **Shape, Space and Measures** P4 Pupils react to and begin to search for objects that have gone out of sight, hearing or touch. They begin to understand position and the relationship between objects, such as stacking or aligning objects. | 4) Pupils should also begin to classify groups by their common feature e.g. • Looking in a box and finding all the objects are red. This could be done by asking pupils to guess the common feature after each object is taken from the box. • Identifying objects by features without seeing them, such as feeling. As all these objects are round, hard and cold, they might be marbles. • Looking at photos of a group of familiar pupils and identifying that they are all in Barry's class. etc. |
| | | P5 Pupils react to and begin to search for objects that are in their usual place. They manipulate positions. They compare one object with another according to its size or length, responding to bigger, smaller, longer, shorter. | 5) Pupils can make use of information technology to label shapes using a simple art package e.g. • Making line drawings of geometrical shapes. • Making big squares and little shapes. • Repeating a sequence of shapes using copying function. • Creating shapes to fill in the gaps between little shapes and big shapes. |
| | | P6 Pupils search for objects not found in their usual location. | |
| 2. The appreciation of pattern | Comparison | **Early Development** P3 Pupils show anticipation in response to familiar people, routines, activities and actions and respond appropriately to | 1) Given a selection of objects the pupil selects those that are similar to complete a task e.g. • Selecting all the bricks for building. • Choosing only the cutlery for a tea party. • Choosing to take out all the footballs for a game rather than just one. etc. |

| Phase | Strand | Level Description | Activities/Programmes of Study |
|---|---|---|---|
| | | them. They explore or manipulate objects, toys or other equipment. They are able to communicate simple choices, likes and dislikes. They can communicate using different tones and sounds and use some vocalisations and/or gestures to communicate.<br><br>**Using and Applying**<br>P5<br>Pupils match with help objects and/or pictures. They group or sort sets of objects by characteristics such as size or shape.<br><br>P6<br>Pupils copy simple patterns or sequences. They sort objects but do not always consistently apply the criterion chosen.<br><br>**Shape, Space and Measures**<br>P4<br>Pupils react to and begin to search for objects that have gone out of sight, hearing or touch. They begin to understand position and the relationship between objects, such as stacking or aligning objects. | 2) The pupil copies actions made by a member of staff in a game situation e.g.<br>• Putting hands on his/her head during 'Simon says'.<br>• Rolling the ball down a slide in skittles.<br>• Joining in the actions to a variety of songs.<br>etc.<br><br>3) In exploring objects the pupil learns that some things look the same but can be very different e.g.<br>• Trying to chew a plastic biscuit or drink some of the vinegar.<br>• Trying to put the milk bottles back into too small a crate.<br>• Trying to throw a medicine ball instead of the football.<br>etc.<br><br>4) The pupil demonstrates an awareness of one-to-one correspondence e.g.<br>• Counting out one straw for each bottle of milk.<br>• Serving one potato for each plate.<br>• Finding one hat for each member of the class to go out in.<br>etc.<br><br>5) The pupil matches one object to another similar object e.g.<br>• Finding the matching shoe or glove to a pair.<br>• Finding the jigsaw piece that fills a gap.<br>• Building a tower of one-coloured bricks from a wide selection.<br><br>6) In using a programmable toy a pupil can make use of two buttons that make two different actions occur, e.g. pressing forward and pressing turn. |

| Phase | Strand | Level Description | Activities/Programmes of Study |
|---|---|---|---|
| | | P5<br>Pupils react to and begin to search for objects that are in their usual place. They manipulate positions. They compare one object with another according to its size or length, responding to bigger, smaller, longer, shorter.<br><br>P6<br>Pupils search for objects not found in their usual location. | 7) Pupils will begin to discard inappropriate materials which they need to complete a task e.g.<br>• Rejecting a kitchen knife in making a picture in art.<br>• Rejecting a paintbrush as a means of operating the computer.<br><br>8) Using an art package on the computer a pupil can 'rubber band' shapes, stretching and squashing them to display how the size of shapes can be altered. |
| 2. The appreciation of pattern | Patterns | **Early Development**<br>P3<br>Pupils show anticipation in response to familiar people, routines, activities and actions and respond appropriately to them. They explore or manipulate objects, toys or other equipment. They are able to communicate simple choices, likes and dislikes. They can communicate using different tones and sounds and use some vocalisations and/or gestures to communicate.<br><br>**Using and Applying**<br>P5<br>Pupils match with help objects and/or pictures. They group | 1) Pupils should be starting to copy simple patterns made by a member of staff. These could occur in any medium e.g.<br>• Copying a rhythmic pattern clap/click/click... etc<br>• Finding a pattern in playing different musical instruments, C/F/G on the xylophone.<br>• Copying a pattern of actions with a member of staff, such as head/shoulders/knees and toes. etc.<br><br>2) A pupil could copy a regular routine that another pupil is following e.g.<br>• One pupil following a physio programme involving lifting his/her legs which a second pupil attempts to imitate.<br>• One pupil being told how to mix a drink, which another pupil copies.<br>• Copying a routine involved in cleaning one's teeth. etc. |

| Phase | Strand | Level Description | Activities/Programmes of Study |
|---|---|---|---|
| | | or sort sets of objects by characteristics such as size or shape.<br><br>**P6**<br>Pupils copy simple patterns or sequences. They sort objects but do not always consistently apply the criterion chosen.<br><br>**Shape, Space and Measures**<br>**P4**<br>They begin to understand position and the relationship between objects, such as stacking or aligning objects.<br><br>**P5**<br>Pupils compare one object with another according to its size or length, responding to bigger, smaller, longer, shorter.<br><br>**P6**<br>Pupils search for objects not found in their usual location. | 3) A pupil should start to indicate that he/she can find a pattern in the environment e.g.<br>• Following a triangular line marked on the table with his/her finger.<br>• Pointing to each tile in turn along the wall.<br>• Laying the table according to a pattern and accompanying the action with words, knife, fork, spoon, knife, fork, spoon.<br>etc.<br><br>4) A pupil can be encouraged to continue a pattern that has already been started e.g<br>• Jumping from one colour mat to another and then to a third and then continuing in time to the music in PE.<br>• Completing a pattern of colours in potato prints in art.<br>• Using a concept keyboard to program a turtle to complete a set number of movements to continue a sequence of squares during IT.<br>etc.<br><br>5) A pupil can organise a set of materials into a number of patterns e.g.<br>• Organising a set of pegs into a multicoloured line.<br>• Building with bricks, a wide brick followed by a narrow brick etc.<br>• Taking a set of stacking rings and organising them according to a decrease in size.<br>etc.<br><br>6) Patterns can be explored through the use of a computer in a variety of ways e.g. |

| Phase | Strand | Level Description | Activities/Programmes of Study |
|---|---|---|---|
| | | | • Pupils can work at creating mosaics using a program such as Tiler (BBC).<br>• Art packages give pupils who can use a mouse or touchscreen the option of exploring ray traced patterns, and learning to flip and rotate shapes. |
| 2. The appreciation of pattern | Estimation | **Early Development**<br>P3<br>Pupils show anticipation in response to familiar people, routines, activities and actions and respond appropriately to them. They explore or manipulate objects, toys or other equipment. They are able to communicate simple choices, likes and dislikes. They can communicate using different tones and sounds and use some vocalisations and/or gestures to communicate.<br><br>**Using and Applying**<br>P5<br>Pupils match with help objects and/or pictures. They group or sort sets of objects by characteristics such as size or shape.<br><br>P6<br>Pupils copy simple patterns or sequences. They sort objects but do not | 1) The child will select an approximate number of blocks to build a tower similar to one which has already been created.<br>• Using Duplo a child selects three bricks to match a tower that is more than one.<br><br>2) The child selects groups of objects when they are aware that there is a need for more than one to share amongst peers e.g.<br>• Taking a handful of straws to distribute to the group to help at drinks time.<br>• Pointing to a tray of milk at drinks time, rather than to a single carton.<br>• Finding a tray of crayons for everyone in the group.<br><br>3) The pupil will choose an appropriate quantity of a material to complete a task e.g.<br>• Taking a tub of soft dough to make a small group of biscuits.<br>• Taking a bottle of milk with sufficient to share with friends.<br>• Mixing enough paint to fill in the picture.<br><br>4) The child seeks to collect enough of a material to match or balance a previously defined group e.g.<br>• Balancing a bag of sand with a similar sized bag of sugar. |

| Phase | Strand | Level Description | Activities/Programmes of Study |
|---|---|---|---|
| | | always consistently apply the criterion chosen.<br><br>**Shape, Space and Measures**<br>P5<br>Pupils react to and begin to search for objects that are in their usual place. They manipulate positions. They compare one object with another according to its size or length, responding to bigger, smaller, longer, shorter.<br><br>P6<br>Pupils search for objects not found in their usual location. With support they make a direct comparison of two masses. They order a set of objects according to their size. | • Taking a suitable sized container with enough water in to balance a jug on the scales.<br>etc. |
| 3. Symbolic | Prediction | **Using and Applying**<br>P6<br>Pupils copy simple patterns or sequences. They sort objects but do not always consistently apply the criterion chosen.<br><br>P7<br>Pupils sort objects, given a criterion such as picking out all the silver coins in | At this level pupils are beginning to move from the prediction of certainties to an understanding of what is most likely to happen.<br>1) Pupils can start by determining outcomes from events e.g.<br>• If it doesn't rain this afternoon, we can go outside.<br>• If the pool is being cleaned later today, then really we can't swim.<br>• If the computer room is free, then we can get our letters typed. |

| Phase | Strand | Level Description | Activities/Programmes of Study |
|---|---|---|---|
| | | a purse. They talk about simple repeating patterns and attempt to recreate them. They begin to use mathematical ideas of matching and sorting to solve simple problems like how to display books on a shelf.<br><br>P8<br>Pupils recognise, describe and recreate simple repeating patterns and sequences. They begin to use their developing mathematical understanding. | 2) Pupils can be assisted in answering questions that expect an either/or response e.g.<br>• If a bag contains Jelly Babies and Liquorice Allsorts, when I take one out it will be one or the other.<br>• Students can make two choices for activities, one for good weather and one for poor weather.<br>• Dice with only two or three symbols on can be used in simple number games to limit the possibilities.<br><br>3) Pupils can also start to identify what is most likely to happen in a given situation e.g.<br>• If my bag contains 99 Smarties and 1 jelly bean, which am I most likely to get when I put my hand in?<br>• If the number 5 bus runs every 15 minutes and the number 6 only once an hour, which bus is likely to come to the stop next? etc.<br><br>4) Pupils should try to record and represent the information upon which their ideas are based.<br>• Sorting out all the sweets in a bag to see which there are most of in the bag, and then deciding which is the most likely to be chosen.<br><br>5) Pupils should also start to recognise that we can suggest what we think is least likely to happen e.g.<br>• It is unlikely that the tortoise will beat the hare in a race.<br>• The scissors are unlikely to be in the drawer marked 'pencils'. |

| Phase | Strand | Level Description | Activities/Programmes of Study |
|-------|--------|-------------------|-------------------------------|
| | | | 6) Pupils should communicate why they believe that something is more or less likely e.g. <br> • There are more Smarties than Jelly Babies in the bag so I will probably get a Smartie. <br> • Clouds often make it rain, and it is cloudy today, so it is likely it will rain. |
| 3. Symbolic | Classification | **Using and Applying** <br> **P6** <br> Pupils copy simple patterns or sequences. They sort objects but do not always consistently apply the criterion chosen. <br><br> P7 <br> Pupils sort objects, given a criterion such as picking out all the silver coins in a purse. They talk about simple repeating patterns and attempt to recreate them. They begin to use mathematical ideas of matching and sorting to solve simple problems like how to display books on a shelf. <br><br> P8 <br> Pupils recognise, describe and recreate simple repeating patterns and sequences. They begin to use their developing mathematical understanding. | 1) Pupils can look at pictorial databases e.g. <br> • Pictures with text under headings. <br> • Making a wall chart or flipbook of facts. <br> • Using software that combines facts within the program, such as Viewpoints (Sherston Software). <br><br> 2) Pupils can make use of open-ended software in which they can create simple files along specific themes. <br><br> Pupils can then search these files for pieces of information. <br><br> Appropriate themes could include: <br> • My house <br> • My street <br> • All about us <br> • Recipes for cooking <br> • Transport <br><br> In using this software, the following could be used: <br> • Ask questions about the facts <br> • Use the format to collect facts <br> • Use the information within a project <br><br> Display the information for others to use in an exhibition, school brochure or guide book. |

| Phase | Strand | Level Description | Activities/Programmes of Study |
|---|---|---|---|
| | | **Space, Shape and Measures**<br>P7<br>Pupils use some familiar words to describe position, size and quantity. They start to pick out particular shapes from a collection: for example, all the circles. They recognise forwards and backwards directions.<br><br>P8<br>Pupils compare directly two lengths or masses and find out by pouring which of two containers holds more or less. They show awareness of time through some familiarity with names of the days of the week and significant times in their day, such as mealtimes, bedtimes. They use mathematical vocabulary such as 'straight', 'circle', 'larger' to describe the shape and size of solids and flat shapes, and use a variety of shapes to make and describe simple models, pictures and patterns. | 3) Pupils can use IT through a concept keyboard or clicker grid to record categories into which objects fall.<br><br>4) Pupils should be using number to describe and classify sets of objects e.g.<br>• The set of three.<br>• The set of lemons with two more than any other.<br>etc. |
| 3. Symbolic | Comparison | **Using and Applying**<br>P6<br>Pupils copy simple patterns or sequences. | 1) Pupils should use number to describe one set of objects in relation to another e.g. |

| Phase | Strand | Level Description | Activities/Programmes of Study |
|-------|--------|-------------------|-------------------------------|
| | | They sort objects but do not always consistently apply the criterion chosen.<br><br>**P7**<br>Pupils sort objects, given a criterion such as picking out all the silver coins in a purse. They talk about simple repeating patterns and attempt to recreate them. They begin to use mathematical ideas of matching and sorting to solve simple problems like how to display books on a shelf.<br><br>**P8**<br>Pupils recognise, describe and recreate simple repeating patterns and sequences. They begin to use their developing mathematical understanding.<br><br>**Shape, Space and Measures**<br>**P7**<br>Pupils use some familiar words to describe position, size and quantity. They start to pick out particular shapes from a collection: for example, all the circles. They recognise forwards and backwards directions. | • Can I have the box of five bricks?<br>• Can I have 100g of flour?<br><br>2) Pupils should use an increasingly complex preposition to describe the position of objects e.g.<br>• The ball is behind the box and in front of the car.<br>• The ball is above and behind the car.<br><br>3) Pupils should use symbols to record the comparisons they make as a shorthand form.<br><br><br><br>= on<br><br>Pupils should sequence objects or symbols appropriately. |

| Phase | Strand | Level Description | Activities/Programmes of Study |
|---|---|---|---|
| | | **P8**<br>Pupils compare directly two lengths or masses and find out by pouring which of two containers holds more or less. They show awareness of time through some familiarity with names of the days of the week and significant times in their day, such as meal times, bed times. They use mathematical vocabulary such as 'straight',' circle', 'larger' to describe the shape and size of solids and flat shapes, and use a variety of shapes to make and describe simple models, pictures and patterns. | |
| 3. Symbolic | Patterns | **Using and Applying**<br>**P6**<br>Pupils copy simple patterns or sequences. They sort objects but do not always consistently apply the criterion chosen.<br><br>**P7**<br>Pupils sort objects, given a criterion such as picking out all the silver coins in a purse. They talk about simple repeating patterns and attempt to | 1) Pupils should be introduced to how shapes might fit together to make patterns e.g.<br>• Using a coloured rectangle and exploring the creation of a repeating pattern.<br>• Exploring making a large mosaic with floor tiles.<br>• Taking shapes to make a reflecting pattern on the wall and anticipating where the two ends will meet.<br><br>2) Pupils can try to find patterns in numbers that will fit a given rule. e.g.<br>• All even numbers on one side, all odd numbers on the other. |

| Phase | Strand | Level Description | Activities/Programmes of Study |
|---|---|---|---|
| | | recreate them. They begin to use mathematical ideas of matching and sorting to solve simple problems like how to display books on a shelf.<br><br>**P8**<br>Pupils recognise, describe and recreate simple repeating patterns and sequences. They begin to use their developing mathematical understanding.<br><br>**Shape, Space and Measures**<br>**P6**<br>Pupils search for objects not found in their usual location, demonstrating their understanding of object permanence. Pupils show understanding of words, signs or symbols that describe positions (for example, by responding to a request to put a pen next to a book or in a pot) and of vocabulary such as 'more' or 'less', when working with quantities. With support, they make a direct comparison of two masses. They order a set of objects | • Numbers beginning with 'S'<br>• Multiples of 3.<br>  etc.<br><br>3) Pupils should discover the beginning and end of patterns in lines of numbers or other components e.g.<br><br>1, 2, 4, 2, 1, 2, 4, 2 etc.<br>1, 2, 3, 3, 2, 1, 1, 2, 3, 3, 2, 1 etc.<br><br>4) Pupils might like to see if they can find mini patterns within larger patterns.<br><br>5) Pupils should start to recognise that a symbol can stand for/represent a missing object.<br>• Pupils could be introduced to number machines both on paper and on computers e.g.<br>2  +1  3  5  +2  7<br>• Pupils should recognise that numbers can be arranged according to simple rules<br>  e.g.  2 x table<br>           3 x table etc. |

| Phase | Strand | Level Description | Activities/Programmes of Study |
|---|---|---|---|
| | | according to their size, showing awareness of the vocabulary 'larger', 'smaller', 'largest', 'smallest'.<br><br>P7<br>Pupils use some familiar words to describe position, size and quantity. They start to pick out particular shapes from a collection: for example, all the circles. They recognise forwards and backwards directions.<br><br>P8<br>Pupils compare directly two lengths or masses and find out by pouring which of two containers holds more or less. They show awareness of time through some familiarity with names of the days of the week and significant times in their day, such as mealtimes, bedtimes. They use mathematical vocabulary such as 'straight', 'circle', 'larger' to describe the shape and size of solids and flat shapes, and use a variety of shapes to make and describe simple models, pictures and patterns. | |
| Phase | Strand | Level Description | Activities/Programmes of Study |

| Phase | Strand | Level Description | Activities/Programmes of Study |
|---|---|---|---|
| 3. Symbolic | Estimation | **Using and Applying** P6 Pupils copy simple patterns or sequences. They sort objects but do not always consistently apply the criterion chosen.<br><br>P7 Pupils sort objects, given a criterion such as picking out all the silver coins in a purse. They talk about simple repeating patterns and attempt to recreate them. They begin to use mathematical ideas of matching and sorting to solve simple problems like how to display books on a shelf.<br><br>P8 Pupils recognise, describe and recreate simple repeating patterns and sequences. They begin to use their developing mathematical understanding.<br><br>**Shape, Space and Measures** P7 Pupils use some familiar words to describe position, size and quantity. They start to pick out particular shapes | 1) Pupils will start to develop a feel for estimation by trying to find groups of objects that are similar in size e.g.<br>• Pupils can serve out a plate of cakes to one table in a cafe, ask other pupils to take a similar number to the next table.<br>• Pupils can sort out the books in the library into similar sized piles.<br>• At lunchtime pupils might get three fish fingers, ask them to serve out a similar number to others in the class.<br>etc.<br><br>2) Pupils can estimate if they need more or less of a material in relation to something that has changed e.g.<br>• If I need this amount of sand to fill a bucket, will I need more or less to fill this smaller one?<br>• If I need this amount of water to fill this square bottle, will I need more or less to fill a round one?<br>• If it takes a whole sheet of wrapping paper to wrap this parcel, will I need more or less to wrap this other different parcel?<br>etc.<br><br>3) Pupils can estimate length by comparison to non-standard measures e.g.<br>• If this book is as wide as your foot, will this next book be as wide or wider than your foot?<br>• If it takes three cupfuls to fill this bottle, will this smaller cup take more or less cupfuls to fill the bottle?<br>• If I need five books to cover this table top, will I need more or less to cover a smaller desk?<br>etc. |

| Phase | Strand | Level Description | Activities/Programmes of Study |
|---|---|---|---|
| | | from a collection: for example, all the circles. They recognise forwards and backwards directions.<br><br>P8<br>Pupils compare directly two lengths or masses and find out by pouring which of two containers holds more or less. They show awareness of time through some familiarity with names of the days of the week and significant times in their day, such as mealtimes, bedtimes. They use mathematical vocabulary such as 'straight', 'circle', 'larger' to describe the shape and size of solids and flat shapes, and use a variety of shapes to make and describe simple models, pictures and patterns. | |
| 3. Symbolic | Number | **Number**<br>P4<br>Pupils show an interest in number rhymes, songs and finger games.<br><br>P5<br>Pupils join in with familiar number rhymes, songs, stories and games. | 1) Identify a set of objects to be counted. When working through classification and comparison activities, try to create a model of counting those within a set, rather than those that fall outside of the set.<br><br>2) Count objects in a set once and once only e.g.<br>• Encourage pupils to remove objects from a set as they count them. |

| Phase | Strand | Level Description | Activities/Programmes of Study |
|---|---|---|---|
| | | They can indicate one or two: for example, using their fingers. | • Play games on the touchscreen where graphics disappear when they are touched. Count out loud as they are pressed. |
| | | **P6** Pupils demonstrate their understanding of one-to-one correspondence. They join in rote counting up to five and use numbers to five in familiar activities or games. They count reliably up to three objects. They demonstrate an understanding of the concept of more/fewer. They use 1p coins in shopping for items up to 5p. They join in with new number rhymes, songs, stories and games with some assistance or encouragement. | 3) Encourage pupils to learn the number names. Use the number names in order regularly. Number rhymes, songs and number games are all useful in practising the names.

4) Use computer software that involves matching numerals to sets and to other numerals. This can be extended to include matching by memory.

5) Use numbers in specific contexts; money and time are possibilities e.g.
• Play with a calculator.
• Use real time and accelerated clocks to relate numbers as quantity to the passage of time.

6) Use numbers within personal diary entries, time/date/place. Extend diaries into personal organisers. |
| | | **P7** Pupils join in rote counting of numbers to ten. They count reliably at least five objects. They make marks to record a number they have counted and begin to recognise numerals from 1 to 5. Pupils begin to use mathematical language such as 'more or less', 'greater or smaller', to compare two | |

| Phase | Strand | Level Description | Activities/Programmes of Study |
|---|---|---|---|
| | | given numbers of objects or counters and say which is more or less, and to find one more and one less.<br><br>P8<br>Pupils join in with rote counting of numbers to beyond ten. They continue the rote count onwards from a given small number. They count reliably at least ten objects, and compare two given numbers of objects, saying which is more and which is less (or fewer). They begin to use ordinal numbers (first, second, third … ) when describing positions of objects, e.g. people in a line. They find one more and one less than a given number of objects. Pupils estimate a small number such as the number of apples in a bowl, and check by counting. They begin to recognise numerals from 0 to 10 and relate them to collections of objects. They are starting to record numerals to represent up to five objects, with some reversals or inaccuracies. | |
| Phase | Strand | Level Description | Activities/Programmes of Study |

# Chapter 4 - Maths and the Wider Curriculum

The unresolved issue of teaching mathematics to pupils who are working primarily within the level 1 programmes of study is that of the key stage at which pupils are working. To overcome some of these challenges it is suggested that the teaching of mathematics in a modular manner based around a theme has two strong advantages.

Firstly, material from the higher key stages can be incorporated at an appropriate level for the individual by means of the theme reflecting the higher key stage. Secondly, the themes used can be developed in such a way as to involve pupils in activities that are appropriate to whatever level or phase within level 1 they are currently working at.

To illustrate this I have drawn up four outline themes, one for each key stage. Pupils cannot of course be learning the full breadth of mathematical understanding within any one of these themes, but if other themes are developed within a key stage then such coverage could be ensured.

The use of themes or integrated schemes of work is well documented in National Curriculum documentation (Curriculum Guidance 9, NCC, 1991). The use of integrated schemes of work to deliver key stage appropriate material has also been suggested in the past, and these examples are intended to examine this possibility in greater detail. Whilst the focus on direct teaching is clear within the National Numeracy Strategy (1999), this should not be seen as precluding the direct teaching of mathematics whilst within a topic that links to other subjects.

For the purposes of this book the themes chosen for development are:

Key Stage 1 - Mazes
Key Stage 2 - Logo and Turtles
Key Stage 3 - Patterns in World Culture
Key Stage 4 - Pyramids

## Key Stage 1 - Mazes

### Outcome
To follow a maze in the school hall, making decisions at key points and recording decisions for later review.

### Programme of study
*Shape, Space and Measures*
- Pupils should be taught to visualise and describe positions, directions and movements using common words.
- Recognise movements in straight lines, translations and rotations and combine them in simple ways.

*Using and applying shape, space and measures*
- Use the correct language and vocabulary associated with shape, space and measures.

### Activities
The maze can take a variety of forms and operate at a variety of levels. At the most basic the maze should simply offer a choice of two directions to achieve a desired goal. (Each line represents a strip of poster paper or carpet laid out upon the floor.)

From this starting point a variety of extra decisions can be added and pupils can begin to record the decisions they have taken. Specific parts of the maze can be colour coded - follow the yellow brick road etc.

Get from ☆ → ✿

### Meeting individual needs

Pupils can use a variety of forms of communication to direct themselves along the maze - an echo 4 communication machine with 'yes' and 'no' can help pupils make choices about directions. Equally pupils can use the maze as an area in which the use of powered wheelchairs can be practised.

More able children can begin the process of designing a maze, starting by adding a path, which allows people to complete the puzzle.

Routes can be recorded in a variety of ways - using a tape player or video recorder to tape the decisions as they are taken and then playing them back using a model to see what other choices might have led to.

### Extension activities

Mazes can lead directly to map work: can we turn the map of the school into a maze?
Outdoor mazes
Planning a maze as part of a 'Dungeons and Dragons' fantasy role-playing maths day

### Resources

Stair carpet rolls
Poster paper rolls
Taped-out paths (similar to laying out a tennis court)

### Step-by-step guide

1. Follow a line - can you walk along a bench - can you drive your chair along this line?
2. Single decisions to achieve an agreed goal
3. Multiple decisions to achieve an agreed goal
4. Planning a route for someone else to follow
5. Planning a maze for someone else to complete
6. Working with computers to design and try mazes

### Teaching style

A range of teaching styles is appropriate to these resources. Simple closed questions, which require pupils with complex needs to use a developing yes/no response, can be used with pupils to support early decision-making skills at an early stage. This can lead into more open-ended questions in planning a route, whereby children with complex needs select from options which route they wish to take, for instance by using a simple four-symbol communication board.

The work that pupils carry out can be individual or in small groups with one or more pupils being directed through the maze by others (The Crystal Maze).

## How long will it take?

Work with mazes can easily fill a term or more on weekly sessions of up to an hour. It can therefore provide a useful activity within some of the elements of the Numeracy Hour with careful planning for progression. Good planning of the use of the school hall is essential.

# Key Stage 2 - Logo and Turtles

## Outcome

To plan a route and to give clear instructions to a computer turtle to complete that route. To explore patterns, distance, to estimate and compare.

## Programme of study

*Shape, Space and Measures*

Key Stage 2

- Understand and use measures.
- Understand and use the properties of shape.
- Understand and use the properties of position and movement.

For detail refer back to Key Stage 1

- Compare objects using common uniform non-standard units and with a standard unit of length.

Compare events with a standard unit of time.

- Describe properties of shape.
- Pupils should be taught to visualise and describe positions, directions and movements using common words.
- Recognise movements in straight lines, translations and rotations and combine them in simple ways.

## Activities

The route can be simple or complex and can be carried out in a variety of ways.

The Turtle can be programmed using Logo and a concept keyboard, or through the use of Clicker can be accessed by switch users.

1. On wallpaper on the floor, how many Turtle presses to reach the finish line?

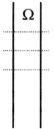

2. Add together Turtle presses to reach line 5 - how many different ways of reaching 5 are there (1+4) (2+3) etc.
3. Play Turtle Skittles: program the Turtle to move and knock down as many skittles as possible; for more advanced users, a second 'bowl' is from where the Turtle stopped after your first set of commands.
4. Design patterns of movements for the Turtle - make the Turtle dance set to music.

## Meeting individual needs

Pupils can access the Turtle through a variety of methods, switches, touchscreen, concept keyboard etc. If this is too difficult, pupils can use a communication aid with a peer facilitating the physical actions.

Pupils can use the Turtle as a source of problems to be solved, what happens if barriers are in the way, can he go uphill etc.

## Extension activities

1. Follow my Turtle - especially good for children learning to use a powered chair for the first time
2. Art and technology - design a shell for the Turtle, can he be a lorry, can he be a ballerina? Can we design a shell that is waterproof etc?

## Resources

PC/Archimedes computer
Variation on Logo (Logotron Software)
Clicker (Crick Computing)
Valiant Turtle
Wallpaper/poster paper

## Step-by-step guide

1. How do we make the Turtle move?
2. Movement in one direction - single moves and combinations
3. Turning 90° and moving in two directions or more
4. Planning a program and testing it out
5. Copying someone else's program
6. Correcting a program when it has gone wrong

## Teaching style

As with the module on Mazes, a variety of teaching styles are accessible in this scheme of work. It is possible to move from closed questions to more open ones within a lesson. Once the foundations have been laid, the work lends itself to an investigative style. Pupils can also begin to take some responsibility for their own learning by using the Turtle in imaginative ways. I have seen excellent art work done by teachers allowing pupils to drive several Turtles through pools of paint onto large sheets of paper.

## How long will it take?

Each session should be around 45 minutes to one hour fitting comfortably within a series of lessons within the Numeracy Hour. It has taken two sessions a week for a term to cover all of the material identified above.

# Key Stage 3 - Patterns in World Culture

**Outcome**

To explore the creation and copying of a range of patterns found through cultures and faiths. To use simple notation to describe these patterns, and then to recreate these.

**Programme of study**

*Key Stage 3 Number and Algebra*
- Sequences
  Find the first terms of a sequence given a rule
- Using and applying number and algebra
  Explore, identify and use pattern and symmetry.

Refer back to Key Stage 1 for detail.

*Using and applying number*
- Communicate in oral, pictorial and written form progressing from informal language and recording to mathematical language and symbols.

*Understanding and using patterns and properties of shape*
- Describe properties of shapes

**Activities**

Patterns have long been part of a range of cultures both in history and in contemporary faiths. Pupils can explore a wide range of these and can use these as the basis of creative work and to explore notions of tessellation, rotation and symmetry.

- Islamic patterns - repeating patterns, continue the pattern, visit a mosque, create a floor pattern
- African patterns - explore painting patterns on our faces and bodies
- Tessellating shapes - how do these shapes fit together?

 Or

- Roman mosaics - use small squares of pottery or paper to make a suitable mosaic of your own. How many tiles are needed to complete an area?

**Meeting individual needs**

The use of multicultural materials in mathematics is a useful way of introducing a wider world to children with complex needs. There are a variety of ways of manipulating the symbols and building blocks to meet needs and larger materials such as logiblocks can be used for children with poor hand function.

In addition there are a range of ways of using computers to create such patterns. For instance, by using the Properties option in Windows 95/98 children can create wallpaper for the screen on a PC. This allows them to personalise their computer in a variety of ways.

Pupils should also have a number of opportunities to describe what they like about a pattern and to express choices and preferences in creating patterns.

**Extension activities**

Patterns are intrinsic to much of our art and culture. Pupils can explore the use of repeating patterns in music. Most pop and rock music is based upon a repeating riff, a riff being a pattern of notes that is repeated and developed. Equally, pupils might like to explore how we use patterns in the west in the twentieth century, in advertising and packaging. Similarly, pupils can explore reflection through simple icons from Christianity and Judaism.

Pupils may also be interested to explore the use of Fractals. There are a number of screen savers for the PC which are based upon Fractal geometry.

**Resources**

Photos and tactile pattern tiles from a variety of cultures (local RE centres may be able to help)
Paint, paper, pottery etc.
Display boards
Face paints
PC with Windows 95 (or modern operating system)

**Step-by-step guide**

1. Find your patterns, using a variety of resources. Museums, mosques, temples and churches are a rich source.
2. Choose a simple symbol from a culture and use it to create a frieze to represent that culture. Record the pattern in notation.
3. Use simple geometric shapes to create patterns in more than one direction. Introduce the idea of tiling and see how some shapes fit together and tessellate.
4. Explore a range of different ways of presenting patterns, on floor, ceiling, walls, on our bodies, etc.

**Teaching style**

Lessons that introduce a range of cultures will need to be based upon some concrete experience. Outside visits provide a useful source of integration possibilities for the special school. The lessons should seek to reach a conclusion with many display opportunities along the way.

Once pupils have mastered some of the basic concepts in using shape and space in this manner they can explore new patterns in open-ended ways.

**How long will it take?**

The development of the skills to use shape in this way may require some intensive intervention in the early stage. They may provide part of the group or individual activities within the Numeracy Hour. Pupils with a visual impairment may wish to explore the development of pattern through tactile tiles, and there will be opportunities for pupils with a variety of needs to combine their patterns in new ways. The most effective sessions observed, introduced the skills intensively for four weeks and then introduced a variety of contexts to use these skills for the rest of the term.

# Key Stage 4 - Pyramids

**Outcome**

Recognition of a pyramid shape and its significance to the Egyptians.

**Programme of study**

*Key Stage 4 Shape, Space and Measures*
• Measures and construction

Refer back to Key Stage 1 for detail.

*Patterns and properties of shapes*
- Describe properties of shapes
- Observe, handle and describe common 2D and 3D shapes

## Activities

Explore the shape of a pyramid. Compare three-sided pyramids to four-sided ones. Combine different pyramids together to see what shapes they can make.

Create a template for making pyramids and compare the plan to the 3D shape.

Explore pyramids in history. Look at pyramids in Egypt and the idea of tombs.

Recap work on Mazes as a route to getting into the centre of a tomb to protect the treasure.

Look at other plans of shapes and compare them to the pyramid.

## Meeting individual needs

Pupils can use a variety of communication methods to point to or select a pyramid from a variety of shapes. At a later stage they can use Clicker, scan and select a pyramid shape from a sequence of 3D shapes on a grid. Pyramids can be used as blocks to build larger pyramids and shapes. Pupils can use their communication skills to design pyramids with different coloured walls etc.

## Extension activities

Photos and Videos of the pyramids: Explain how they were used as burial chambers.

Investigate devices to lift and drop gates and doors using sand chambers: Explain how only stone could be used.

Where can we find pyramids in the UK? The Point Cinema at Milton Keynes is one example, as is the Oasis Leisure Centre at Bedford.

## Resources

Card shape
Ruler
Pencil
Plastic kits that can make pyramid shapes e.g. Polygons

## Step-by-Step guide

1. Find a pyramid shape from other shapes.
2. Find other shapes from a collection of pyramids.
3. Make a pyramid.
4. Design and make a container using a pyramid shape.
5. See how pyramids were used in Ancient Egypt.

## Detail

To make a plan of the shape before making a pyramid:
1. Use a solid pyramid and unfold its shape. Remake the solid pyramid.
2. Place the pyramid in different orientations in a sequence. Copy the sequence, then create own sequence.
3. Try to stand the pyramid on its point. Will it stand?

## Teaching style

Open-ended and small group work is ideal for these lessons. There are real opportunities to use IT skills in an intensive way although the activity could be done equally well using card, paper and scissors.

**How long will it take?**

This module can be taken across a series of lessons initially as a core part of the Numeracy Hour. Later it may be used as part of the introduction to recap on previous learning, depending on the ability of the teacher to think creatively and the ability of the pupils to sustain interest in the pyramids.

## Differentiating a single lesson through the Spiral Maths Curriculum

The extended programmes of study have detailed the sorts of activities that can offer a valid mathematical content to children with severe or profound and multiple learning difficulties working within level 1. In addition we have explored some examples of schemes of work which will offer an age-appropriate mathematical context for all pupils.

However, in the classroom we are usually not working with a group of pupils who are all functioning at the same level. It has been suggested that one means of dealing with this is through the use of aims being set in a variety of areas and pupils accessing whichever aim is most relevant to them in the group setting.

There will be occasions when it is of value for all pupils in a small group to be exploring mathematical concepts at their own level, whilst contributing to a co-operative activity. The three phase approach to the spiral curriculum offers us a route by which differentiation can take place.

The following activity demonstrates this principal by providing an example in the form of a lesson plan that has been differentiated to meet the needs of a group of pupils working together, although at different phases of the spiral curriculum.

## Fruit Machine Game

### Outcome

To design and make a random image machine based on the arcade fruit machine, in order to introduce concepts of probability.

### Programme of study

*Handling Data at Key Stage 3*

Pupils should be taught to:
- Appreciate the unpredictability of random processes.
- Explore connections in maths and look for cause and effect.

### Activity
- Make a single drum fruit machine with two different fruit - the 'reel' can be extended to include more fruit for more able pupils.
- Using the single drum and attaching different strips of paper, record what the pupil 'predicts' the outcome will be when the drum is revolved.
- Repeat using greater numbers of different fruit. Are the pupils' predictions correct?

### Meeting individual needs
### Phase 1

Pupils at the earliest stage of development discover that by touching the drum movement occurs and different patterns emerge from the fruit. By filling the drum with pebbles or sand this

50

relationship between action and outcome is reinforced. With just two fruit, the pupil spins the drum and tries to predict what would happen when the drum/wheel/disc stops (use pictures/actual fruit for indicating outcome).

*Phase 1 Prediction*

## Phase 2

Using two or more fruit, keep a record of which fruit face up, can the pupil see any pattern, how can any small pattern be recorded?

*Phase 2 Predictions and patterns*

## Phase 3

Increasing difficulty; can the pupil predict what fruit will appear when two are the same and one is not? Do they choose the most likely one to show? If not do they learn which one it is?

*Phase 3 Prediction/probability*

## Extension activities

Pupils can design their own fruit machine on the computer introducing:

a) predictable outcomes i.e. fixed sequence

and at a later stage

b) random outcomes.

This could be further extended on the computer using exercises created on a program such as ScreenPlay or Powerpoint where a picture/story is animated to run through a set number of times. A different clip can be introduced at a random point in the process.

Does the pupil notice the difference?

Indicates by pressing a switch to continue the program.

## Resources

Large wooden drum (like a tombola drum)

Photos/drawings/paintings of fruit (or it could be any subject the teacher and pupil choose)

## Teaching style

This activity works well with pairs with a fairly high level of teacher direction initially, which is gradually withdrawn.

## How long will it take?

This activity once prepared is ideal for short regular sessions. I have seen it used effectively as part of a teacher's preparation for wet play time.

# The wider perspective

Mathematics, like all learning, is not simply learnt in the classroom. As a teacher in a residential school I was fully aware that there were many rich opportunities for children to develop and build upon their mathematical understanding in the activities planned and delivered in the evenings and weekends.

There are, of course, a variety of ways in which this might happen. Firstly, there are planned non-mathematical activities that draw upon the use of mathematical skills for children to succeed.

**Example - Sports club**

A group of pupils are taking part in a especially adapted ten-pin bowling club. Each pupil must take it in turns to bowl and knock down as many skittles as possible. Scores are kept by building towers equal to the number knocked down. At the end of the game the pupils compare the towers that have been built and choose the pupil with the tallest tower as the winner.

In this activity pupils must draw upon skills of comparison and estimation to select the winner.

Secondly, there are other activities which parents and carers contribute to the experience of the child which are unplanned and offer other opportunities for learning.

**Example - Bath time**

Possibly the classic example of this type of incidental learning can be seen at bath time with a young child. A mother without any prompting will play finger and toe games with the baby. Counting fingers, pointing at body parts etc.

The mother has not gone into the bathroom with any great intention of teaching, merely to get the spaghetti out of her daughter's hair, but the opportunities offered by the interactions are taken.

A third example of the relationship between home and school for learning can be seen in the phenomenon of homework in mainstream schools. The IMPACT maths scheme (Introducing Mathematics to Parents, Children and Teachers) developed at the Polytechnic of North London by Ruth Merttens and Jeffrey Vass has been successfully used as the basis of mathematical activity in special schools. IMPACT suggests a variety of ways in which the work carried out at home can enhance learning in the school, and vice versa. In the IMPACT model, mathematical activities are carried out at both home and school, and an interrelationship between the two is developed.

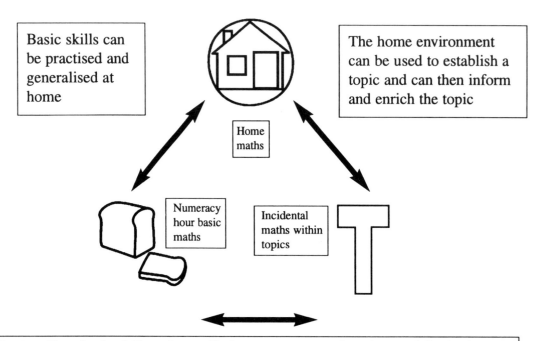

Basic skills can be practised and generalised at home

The home environment can be used to establish a topic and can then inform and enrich the topic

Home maths

Numeracy hour basic maths

Incidental maths within topics

Topics allow basic skills to be applied across a range of settings, whilst basic maths allows practical activities to be reinforced and new concepts introduced

Whilst the materials were developed in mainstream schools, there have been a number of schools that have successfully adapted many of the activities to be accessible to children with special needs. These have included simplified activities, the addition of symbols and paired activities carried out with a sibling in the home.

The National Numeracy Strategy (1999) (pp15-16) also recommends the development of home-school links in delivering the maths curriculum, noting that not all homework and out of school activity need be written. Like the IMPACT project, the value of game puzzles and investigations is highlighted.

The activities offered lay great emphasis upon being active and, like McConkey and McEvoy's 'Count Me In', allow all members of the family to be involved.

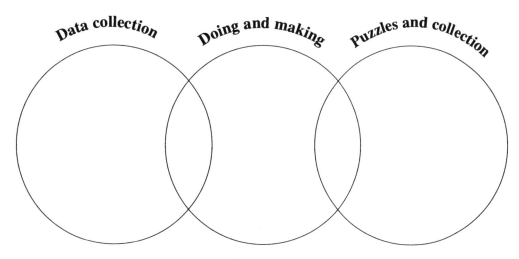

**IMPACT activity types**

Appendix 1 includes three examples of these activities for teachers to adapt. I have used these materials over many years, and reproduce my own favourite here, "Measure Your Pet" (see overleaf), adapted to provide access to symbol users, despite the reactions of colleagues over the years as to what my classes might have done to their hamster, goldfish etc. in the security of their own homes.

## Measure a pet

Can you find a pet to measure?

You will need to use the string.

Stretch the string from your pet's nose to the end of its tail.

Now cut it off.

(The string NOT the pet's tail!)

stretch it around your pet's tummy.

    +

label both pieces of string - tummy and length

Bring both pieces of string to school.

Bring a photo or drawing of your pet.

# Equal opportunities

Mathematics is multicultural. The history of mathematics draws from a diversity of cultures from the Middle East, Africa and the Far East. Many mathematics lessons, however, take little or no account of this rich heritage.

Earlier in the book we looked at a variety of number systems to illustrate the complexity of understanding number. One of the worked examples in Chapter 5 is based around the theme of patterns in world culture. In the example, key algebraic principles are illustrated through repeating patterns from different cultures and faiths.

A further example can be found in finger counting.

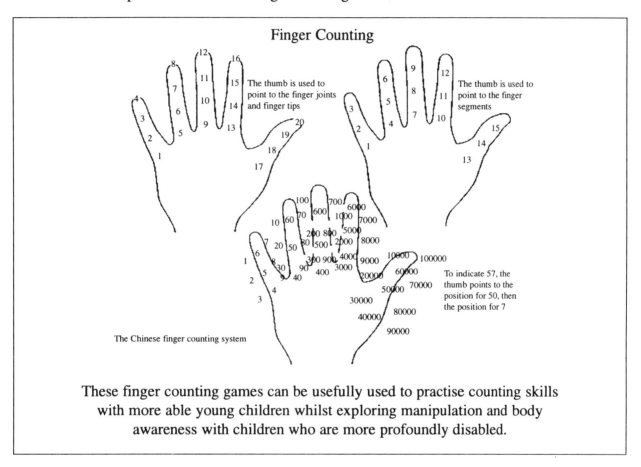

## Finger Counting

The thumb is used to point to the finger joints and finger tips

The thumb is used to point to the finger segments

The Chinese finger counting system

To indicate 57, the thumb points to the position for 50, then the position for 7

These finger counting games can be usefully used to practise counting skills with more able young children whilst exploring manipulation and body awareness with children who are more profoundly disabled.

# Mathematics across the curriculum

The examples above illustrate the ways in which mathematics can play a role in the wider school curriculum, both in establishing links between home and school and in supporting a multicultural approach to education.

I have already argued that mathematics can take place in all activities, in a PE lesson, in science, during therapy. This is further suggested within the National Numeracy Strategy (1999, pp16-17). Mathematics is pervasive throughout the curriculum and there are ample opportunities for any professional working with a child to identify mathematical opportunities in their work. The Spiral curriculum model discussed provides us with a structure by which development in mathematics regardless of context can be charted and aims set.

Additionally we have looked at the creation of a range of mathematical contexts that are directly drawn from the key stage programmes of study and which provide a basis for differentiation of mathematical outcomes.

It would, however, be wrong to suggest that these contexts will always promote mathematical development in all children. The activities suggested are designed to offer rich opportunities for children to develop skills across the curriculum.

In the suggested modules, children have been seen to make achievements in all skill areas. Schools have distinguished between a richness of contexts and specific content. Thus in one of the mathematics lessons children may have shown development in one of eight skill areas.

These skill areas have variously been drawn from key skills, the desirable outcomes or the National Record of Achievement. A list might comprise:

Communication
Literacy
Numeracy
PSE
IT
Study
Problem Solving
Physical

These skill areas are then fully integrated into all areas of the National Curriculum and the wider curriculum.

## Mathematics can be fun!

The theory described in this book is firmly rooted in the practical experience of teachers and mathematics co-ordinators over the past ten years. Throughout that time, in training and supporting teachers, I have stressed the need to motivate children fully to want to learn mathematics. Teachers have responded to this in a number of ways: the use of activities such as those suggested by IMPACT, the development of mathematics games both from schemes and from other classroom resources, and most recently the development of maths trails.

There are some excellent resources available to support the development of a mathematics trail for children. Particular use can be made of Zoë Rhydderch-Evans' *Mathematics in the School Grounds* (1995). In her book she highlights a number of reasons for making use of school grounds, many of which can be applied to the use of maths trails.

Using school grounds to support mathematics can then promote:

Problem solving
Investigation
Discussion
Communicating mathematically
Applying mathematics

There is much to be said for the motivation of getting out of the classroom as well. Maths trails should seek to offer new contexts in which any of the mathematical strands can be practised. What is necessary is that care is taken to make the trail attractive, with accessible instructions which present mathematical concepts in concrete contexts. At Meldreth Manor we have a large site and one of the pages of our trail is reproduced below.

Find these patterns on learning curves:

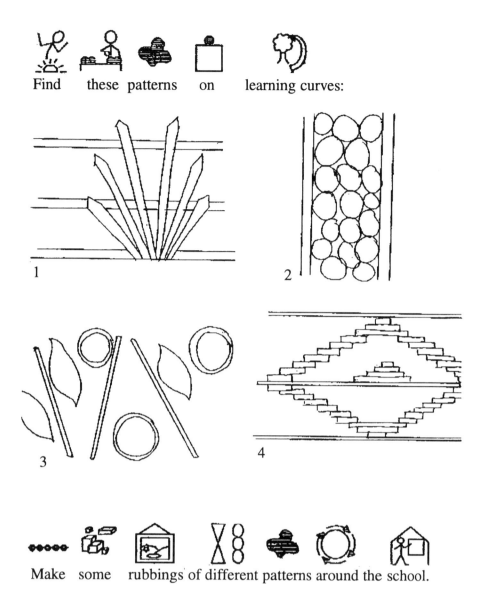

Make some rubbings of different patterns around the school.

At the core of this page of work is that children will have fun outside, they can practise a range of skills including observation (study), hand control (physical) and comparison (numeracy), and that the materials are presented clearly, in an uncluttered manner with symbols to augment and make text accessible.

# Chapter 5 - School Policy and the Role of the Co-ordinator

The National Numeracy Strategy (DfEE, 1999) lays down details of good practice that are useful in informing both the development of policy and the implications for the mathematics co-ordinator. Amongst other points it recommends:

- A co-ordinator for mathematics has the expertise, opportunity and support needed to influence practice.
- There is a whole school approach to the professional development of teachers and other staff involved in the teaching of mathematics.
- There is a daily dedicated mathematics lesson in every class.
- The teaching programme is based upon identified learning outcomes.

Taking these points into account, it is of use to consider the issues of policy and co-ordinator role.

## Mathematics policy

It is not the purpose of this book to examine in depth the process by which a mathematics policy can be developed. However, in working with teachers and co-ordinators from both mainstream and special schools, a range of formats and ideas have been gradually collated.

In addition, the National Numeracy Strategy documentation has a range of guidance to support schools in responding to some of these questions.

In attempting to draw together this disparity we have found the following headings to be useful.

### 1. Nature of the subject

Why is mathematics important to the pupils within any one school, and what is the aim and purpose of the mathematics curriculum? This should link clearly to the values and ethos of the school.

For instance, a school mission statement may speak of the need to promote achievement through self-esteem to maximise the independence of each pupil. In the consideration of the subject, teachers and other staff may well then have drawn clear links between mathematical skills and the ability to solve problems and handle information in the real world.

### 2. A summary of the National Curriculum themes

Many schools have developed a lack of breadth in covering all aspects of the programmes of study. A succinct summary of the strands at each key stage can be useful for teachers who may move from year to year to different parts of the school.

### 3. Progression and continuity

A short summary of the curriculum model used in school and the mathematical strands in which individual aims will be set may be valuable.

In this section one can refer to the ways in which planning and recording will take place in mathematics, and the expectations of the school as to what will be recorded and how.

A clear distinction can be made at this point between the development of skills across the National Curriculum, and the recording of achievements within the cross-curricular skill of numeracy.

## 4. Resources

One of the more pressing problems that schools must grapple with is how resources are to be allocated across the school. Schools may well have adopted a business planning approach by which budget holders are expected to prepare bids for funding of development plans as the school prepares for the new financial year. This is often a useful means by which managers can determine priorities and successfully allocate limited resources.

Within a school policy it is, however, extremely useful to suggest how those limited resources are maximised within the school and within the subject. Materials may be collected across the curriculum within themes or there may be a collection of specific mathematics resources. Distinctions may need to be made between a core of materials that are required within each classroom, or whether some resources are to be maintained and held centrally. This may be a big box in the co-ordinator's cupboard or a fully equipped mathematics base. Whatever is appropriate, the policy should seek to define how resources will be made available to promote learning.

## 5. The role of the co-ordinator

In seeking to promote a successfully implemented mathematics curriculum, the co-ordinator will be a critical factor. It may not be enough to simply have a generic job description for all co-ordinators. The tasks of an IT co-ordinator are likely to be quite different to those of the art co-ordinator or the person with responsibility for maths. It can be useful, however, to attempt to specify the responsibilities of a co-ordinator in relation to staff training, resource management, the review process and liaison with external agencies or parents.

A working policy from Meldreth Manor School along these lines and within the framework of this book is attached as Appendix 2.

# Resourcing the mathematics curriculum

One of the key roles that the co-ordinator must consider is the resources that the school should utilise to effectively deliver the curriculum. For many teachers this will be one of the first ways in which they have been asked to plan in a more strategic manner.

Much of the mathematics that one would wish to deliver will make use of materials that most teachers will find around their shelves anyway. It is useful for the mathematics co-ordinator to ask teachers what it is that they do use in their schemes of work and lessons to clarify the breadth of resources required for all teachers. Some obvious things will no doubt appear - sand, paints, building blocks etc. Some less obvious whole curriculum resources are likely to be identified - communication machines, rebus files, switches, TV or video etc.

There will also be specific mathematical resources identified, which will be needed if one is to resource the curriculum to offer a rich and varied range of mathematical contexts. A list of the types of equipment that might be of value can be found in Appendix 3.

Such a list, however, has only limited validity, as it reflects the needs of specific schools in choosing the manner in which they will deliver all the aspects of the programmes of study for mathematics.

In examining the issues of resources for mathematics in the curriculum, it is still useful to look closely at the range of maths schemes that are available. I would not wish to recommend one or any other, but I have found most successful in schools those schemes which combine both structured work and a variety of games to offer a breadth of activity to children.

As such I have seen successful use of HBJ Maths, Ginn, Maths Chest and Maths Quest in a variety of schools. This has been where those schemes supplement and build upon other approaches. Where there is an over-reliance upon the scheme, there has been less success in the mathematics curriculum.

The other key area of mathematics resources is the use of information technology. The advent of faster Pentium-based computer technology has opened up a variety of materials for children with a special need, and in addition technology can be much utilised as an enabler supporting access to the curriculum through augmentative and alternative communication.

Although it is not entirely appropriate to explain this within the confines of a book on maths, it is useful to comment that as computers become faster and able to handle more instructions per second, so they can run two or more programs simultaneously. This allows computers to handle much more refined graphics or sounds as well as running programs in the background that allow children to use switches and so forth to facilitate access.

There is much to be said for ensuring that a key role of the mathematics co-ordinator is to audit school resources and establish a purchasing plan to deliver a full and varied mathematics curriculum. One of the key techniques for doing this may involve the co-ordinator in examining individual teachers' schemes of work, then collating a list of the resources used. From this starting point the co-ordinator can then examine the full breadth of the programmes of study and identify any gaps between the practice contained in the framework and the practice of teachers within the school.

Other techniques may be to use meeting time to discuss the resources that people use and those they feel they lack. The focus of any such discussion should be on what activities can be delivered through these resources that cannot be adequately delivered today. Questionnaires have been used effectively in schools, but one must beware simply asking team members to fill out yet another form!

## Curriculum monitoring and evaluation

For most co-ordinators monitoring the quality of the curriculum as it is delivered is extremely difficult. Three key components are critical: examining a sample of the work that has been completed by pupils, looking at the teacher's planning, and then considering the teacher's recording of the activity and the pupils' achievements.

In addition it is of great value to the co-ordinator to have access to lesson observations that have been carried out in maths by managers or advisors to the school.

There are a number of ways in which this can be achieved. However, it is important to present information succinctly and in a consistent manner across teachers and subjects.

# Chapter 6 - Future Developments

There remain a wide range of issues that can be developed over the coming years. Whilst there is a need for further work to be done to produce detailed schemes of work which relate one to the other, I believe it likely that much of this work will need to be carried out at school level. There are, however, a number of key areas that require a more co-ordinated approach across schools and authorities. I have divided these into three areas.

• *In-service training needs*

The in-service training programme for teachers in implementing the National Numeracy Strategy has provided a firm basis for further development in schools. There is little doubt that many teachers would value the opportunity to look at the relationship between mathematics and children with special educational needs in much greater detail. The relationship between language acquisition and the development of mathematical skills is one area, which teachers note that assistance would be of value. This is especially true when pupils' language is primarily symbolic (rebus/bliss etc.) and the use of these symbols fundamentally changes the nature of mathematical problems being presented.

Equally the general feelings of unease that I described at the front of this book suggest that there is a need for a much greater understanding of mathematical concepts amongst teachers so that such concepts can be adequately differentiated for pupils. To this end the training to support the National Numeracy Strategy is only a beginning.

• *IT support for mathematics*

The steady move in special education towards a PC platform for IT use in schools, leaves schools with a number of difficulties. There is as yet little directly accessible software for mathematics that would allow for pupils to generate graphs, tables and so forth through the use of a single switch. If a more fully realised integration of mathematics and IT in the special school is to occur then such software will need to be developed.

Equally the preponderance of complex multimedia titles to support the curriculum has presented a number of problems for teachers of children who are switch users, as little of this software is directly accessible. The same challenges are present in giving pupils access to information via the World Wide Web.

• *Development of commercial schemes accessible to non-readers*

In mainstream schools there is a great deal of excellent material available to support the planning and delivery of mathematics schemes of work published by commercial developers. Examples include Maths Chest, Maths Quest and HBJ Mathematics. However, it is often difficult for symbol users to make use of these materials as the text is often inaccessible and diagrams cluttered. There is clearly a need across schools for high-quality materials to be developed that require limited reading skills, or which are supported through symbol systems.

## Conclusion

All pupils regardless of ability have the right to a full and appropriate mathematics curriculum. That curriculum must reflect the needs of the individual, and contain a planned route for progression. The Spiral Mathematics curriculum described above details a curriculum planned along these lines. This means that pupils should be working from the bottom level upwards, starting from the simplest level through to the highest. These themes can be worked on by a mixed ability group. Each theme which we have shown is differentiated to a wide range of abilities. This is based upon sound classroom expertise.

Information technology can provide both access to the initial stages of the curriculum, and access to a greater breadth of curricular experience for all pupils. The use of IT can also support teachers in linking together different areas of the curriculum, National Curriculum, developmental curriculum and therapy. The ideas contained in this curricular model recognise the overlap in the special school curriculum and moreover the interdisciplinary nature of the work in which we are all involved.

Within the National Curriculum there are levels at which our pupils are extremely unlikely to achieve. (If they did, perhaps they are in the wrong place!) Most pupils with severe learning difficulties are likely to be working from within level 1, to a few achieving success at level 3. When working with pupils with PMLD the need to address the entitlement to have a broad and continuous curriculum appropriate to their needs and age has been a primary concern.

In addition, we have been very aware that newer technologies are extremely expensive. Such technology may also not be within the competence of all staff, and so we have attempted to describe a variety of levels of technology that can be effectively used by teachers. We hope that this will assist teachers in identifying the next step in looking to new technology, but hope we also validate the excellent work being done by staff on technology that may be past its sell-by date, but which is facilitating effective learning in the classroom.

This material can only scratch the surface of the development of an effective mathematics curriculum, but we hope it is of value to staff in developing their curriculum further.

Finally, if there is one real need that I have been made aware of over the past five years it is that schools and the staff working within them need time to reconsider the place of mathematics in the curriculum. If there is to be a period of stability in government revisions to schools then this may provide the opportunity for this work to take place.

# Appendix 1 - A Training Pack for Teachers

## Developing teachers to develop mathematics

The purpose of these materials is to provide some inset activities to support the issues that have been raised throughout this book. All of the activities have been tried on a range of audiences over an extended period. In particular the activities have been used by maths co-ordinators in special schools as part of an introduction to maths and mathematics schemes of work.

## Definitions of mathematics - overcoming maths panic

The purpose of this activity is for teachers to have an opportunity to discuss their own perceptions of mathematics and reach an agreed consensus on what we might mean by mathematics in schools for children with severe learning difficulties.

**Activity**

Look at the following definitions of mathematics.

Mathematics may be defined as the subject in which we never know what we are talking about, nor whether what we are saying is true.

(Bertrand Russell, 1872-1970, British philosopher, mathematician)

In a letter of March 1912 to Lady Offoline Morrell, Russell wrote:

'I like mathematics because it is not human and has nothing particular to do with this planet or with the whole accidental universe - because, like Spinoza's God, it won't love us in return.'

Ohp 1

Mathematics isn't a science -
It's a religion
All of these maths books
are full of things that have
to be accepted by faith -
equations, formulae, algebra.
I'm a maths atheist!

(With apologies to Bill Watterstone)

Ohp 2

Can you now complete the
following in less than
12 words -
Mathematics is …

Compare the results with the
definitions that have been
proposed earlier in this book

# Understanding algebra

## People patterns

Take a group of colleagues and choose one to stand at the front of the group. Position this person carefully taking care to decide which way they face, where their hands are placed, what expression you want them to maintain etc. Then select a second person to stand alongside the first and to be positioned differently. Gradually increase the line of people positioning each in turn to create a pattern according to a predetermined criterion that you are working to.

Members of the group who are not selected should attempt to define the rule to which you are working.

For instance, the rule might be male/female, or smile/frown.

The rules of algebra should be explained to the group as they are encountered.

## Design a maths trail for colleagues

After a series of inset sessions exploring the value of mathematics being fun and the value of context in mathematics, it can be valuable for a group to attempt to put these into practice. An evening spent designing a trail for colleagues along the lines of a treasure hunt will illustrate many points from discussion.

Useful points to stress are that:

- The trail must make use of all aspects of mathematics.
- The trail should be accompanied by diagrams.
- The trail must be timed.
- The trail should incorporate both open and closed questions.
- The trail should be fun.

The staff trail should then be developed further for use by pupils. Some examples of trail pages are given below.

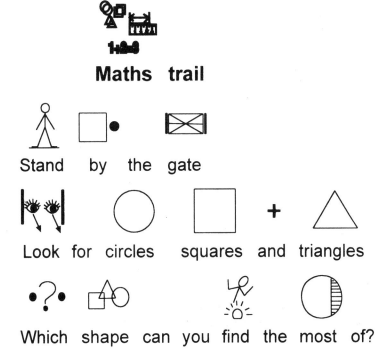

**Maths trail**

Stand by the gate

Look for circles squares and triangles

Which shape can you find the most of?

# The Riding School

How many   horses   do you   think   you   will   find?

Count   the   horses.   How good   was   your   guess?

 =

Horses   are   measured   in   hands.

Ask   the   riding school   teachers   how many   hands   a   horse.

Look   around

What   else   can   you   measure   in   hands?

## Language and mathematics

One of the key features of good mathematics teaching is that it is discussion-based. This popular activity based on an example from the IMPACT Maths scheme is based upon the use of discussion. At the end of the lesson the teacher should use 'Writing with Symbols' (Widgit software) to design a similar sheet to achieve this purpose for children communicating through rebus.

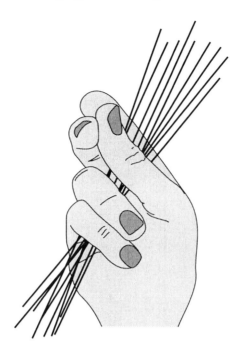

You will need a handful of dried spaghetti.
If you want you could use small bricks or macaroni.
Show your friends how many pieces you have in
your hand.
Put your hand behind your back.
Drop some of your pieces onto the floor.
Show your hand to your friends again.
Can they guess how many you dropped?

Play this game three times each.
If you get the number right you get one point.
The winner is the person with the most points.

# Learning to count

Learning to count is complicated and few teachers actually appreciate the complexity of the task that is provided for pupils. To illustrate the point we will explore some alternative number systems from around the world and the difficulties that abstraction provides.

Use these number squares to create some simple mathematical problems. Ask teachers to solve the problems, first without the key and then with it. Equally ask them to give answers that are translated into our own number system or in one of the other systems.

**Chinese**

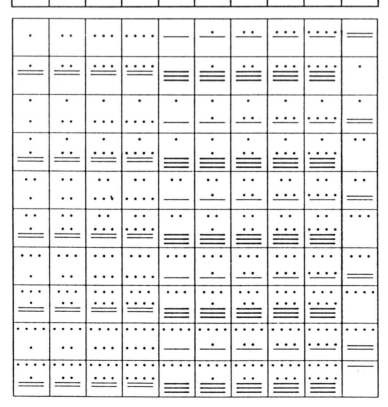

**Mayan**

70

# Multicultural mathematics

Here are some patterns drawn from Islam and Hinduism. Explore the patterns, cut them up and find new patterns you can create that use the elements of these.

**The Shri Yantra**

**Swastika**

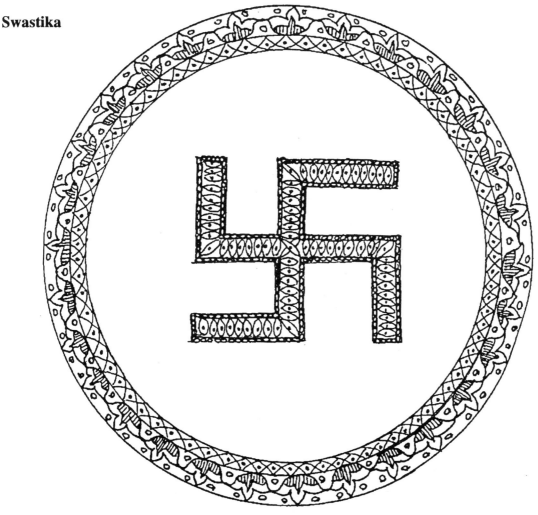

Examine each of the patterns and then plan a lesson using one or more of them. This lesson should use the resource to explore issues of reflection or rotation or symmetry.

Here are some more examples:

# Appendix 2 - Sample Maths Policy (from Meldreth Manor School)

## Policy on mathematics

### 1. Nature of subject

Mathematics is important to all pupils. It provides a means of viewing and making sense of the world and of appreciating the relationships between parts of that world and the structures those parts create. Mathematics has the capacity not only to describe, but also to predict and to explain. For pupils of all abilities therefore, mathematical skills are essential in the development of independence and decision making as pupils begin to understand the world in which they live.

### 2. Mathematics and the National Curriculum

Mathematics is one of the three core subjects of the National Curriculum. At Meldreth Manor School, it is planned at the age appropriate key stage through Integrated Schemes of Work and specific mathematics modules of work. The breadth of the Mathematics Curriculum varies at each key stage:

**Key Stage 1**

    Using and Applying Mathematics
    Number
    Shape, Space and Measures

**Key Stage 2**

    Using and Applying Mathematics
    Number
    Shape, Space and Measures

**Key Stages 3 & 4**

    Using and Applying Mathematics
    Number
    Shape, Space and Measures
    Handling Data

Mathematics is also a crucial area of the curriculum beyond the statutory school years, and is a fundamental part of the FE curriculum.

### Mathematics Across the Whole Curriculum

The application of mathematics across the whole curriculum of the school falls within the cross-curricular skill of numeracy. A summary of the key principles of the skill area is contained within Appendix 1 to this policy. All pupils should have individual goals set within the cross-curricular skill.

### 3. Approaches to Teaching

The curriculum model for mathematics applied at Meldreth Manor School builds upon that suggested in Curriculum Guidance 9, as suggested by the National Curriculum Council. This is referred to as the Spiral Mathematics Curriculum.

All pupils learning mathematics at Meldreth Manor School should demonstrate clear progress and achievement. This can be demonstrated in one of two ways:

## 1. Vertical Progression

This is the traditional model and can be defined as a series of small steps leading to achievements at each of the level descriptions of the National Curriculum for Mathematics.

Examples of such a small step model to assist in setting goals can be found in *Maths for All* (MEC Teacher Fellows, 1991) and the NICC *Stepping Stones to Level 1*, published by the Northern Ireland Curriculum Council.

## 2. Horizontal Progression

This form of progression can take two forms, first that of pupils practising and generalising skills across an increasingly wide range of contexts, and second that which occurs due to the interrelationship between the mathematical concepts in the National Curriculum. It is in the nature of mathematics that the skills and concepts from one strand form the basis of development within other strands as they evolve and become more complex.

## Differentiation

Applying the three levels of the spiral model can hence differentiate a single mathematical activity drawn from the programmes of study for mathematics:

## Phase 1 - Introduction/Foundation

The curriculum for mathematics at this level is concerned with the development of three strands of mathematical learning:

Prediction and Anticipation
Classification
Comparison

The development of these concepts will be related to an introduction to shape and space, moving purposefully in a given direction and rotating oneself to gain a different perspective upon the world. In making comparisons between objects, pupils will begin to have an understanding of quantity, one and more than one, more and less, etc.

## Phase 2 - The Appreciation of Pattern

As pupils develop the skills described above, they will begin to develop an understanding of pattern. This is described within the programmes of study as being part of the development of algebra. The curriculum described within phase 1 is thus extended and now encompasses:

Patterns
Predication and Anticipation
Classification
Comparison
Estimation

In extending the skills they have developed in relation to quantity, pupils will be expected to make early estimates of quantity and size.

## Phase 3 - The Symbolic Level

The third phase of development in early mathematics is concerned with the discovery and use of a variety of means of describing and communicating findings in mathematics. It is at this stage, that pupils may be introduced to concepts such as number and probability. The mathematics curriculum will now encompass the full range of mathematical concepts described within the National Curriculum leading to level 1.

## 4. Access and Progression/Planning and Recording

Each pupil will have individual aims for numeracy set at the Annual Review. The progression identified above is one by which staff can identify the appropriate form of access to the breadth of mathematical ideas. For instance, when teaching Patterns in World Culture, the teacher may wish to judge whether a pupil has access at phases 1, 2 or 3 as an aid to lesson planning, as well as having previously identified the pupil outcomes as Numeracy, Physical Skills, Social Skills, etc.

Pupil achievement in mathematics is recorded under the skill area of Numeracy and recorded in the National Record of Achievement (NRA).

## 5. Organisation and Provision of Resources

Mathematics can be taught in a variety of ways:

*Mathematics Lessons* - in these lessons, mathematics is the basis of the lesson and may be specifically related to any of the strands of mathematics identified previously, e.g. a road traffic survey.

*Incidental Mathematics* - in these lessons, mathematics is not the primary focus of the session, but clear mathematical content can be identified, e.g. a shopping trip.

The provision of resources will vary according to the needs of pupils. Some equipment will be shared across the whole school, such as a Turtle. Other equipment will need to be budgeted for at unit level and should include equipment for measuring, die, logiblocks, scales, etc.

## 6. Role of Subject Co-ordinator

*Professional Development*
   a) Map out the coverage of the mathematics programmes of study at all key stages.
   b) Lead training and development for staff in developing the use of the curriculum model and individual understanding of mathematics.
   c) Plan training in the use of mathematical resources, and identify appropriate resources as and when they are made available.

*Review Process*
   a) Undertake to periodically review goal setting in the area of numeracy.
   b) Review curriculum guidelines, teaching ideas and resources.
   c) Support colleagues in planning and meeting individual needs in mathematics.

*Resources Management*
   a) Build up a central resource of mathematical activities and materials for use throughout the school.
   b) Produce guidelines and advice on planning to meet needs through the use of Spiral model described above.
   c) Produce a Budget Plan to identify key expenditure on an annual basis.

*Liaison with Parents, Governors and Outside Agencies*
   a) Support parents with ideas for mathematical activities to trial at home.
   b) Demonstrate quality of curriculum model to Governors' Curriculum Sub-committee.
   c) Lead professional development beyond the school both locally and nationally.

# Appendix 3 - Resource Materials

The following is a list of mathematical resource materials that builds upon the one offered by Bedfordshire LEA via their excellent Mathematics Resource Centre at Putteridge Bury.

Abaci
Balances (scales)
Calculators and software for PC
Clixi
Compasses
Construction materials - Lego, Sticklebricks etc.
Dice with variety of number of sides and with numerals/dots/shapes etc.
Geoboards
Measures - rulers 30cm, 1 metre etc.
Hoops
Logiblocks
Metric capacity measures
Mirrors
Money
Pattern blocks
Egg timers
Stop watch
Pendulum
Playing cards
Protractors
Sand and water play materials
2D and 3D shapes
Dienes cubes
Tesselating shapes
Trundle wheels

This range of materials is available from a number of suppliers. Many have been available through the following over the past three years.

Hope Education
Orb Mill, Huddersfield Rd, Oldham, Lancs OL4 2ST

LDA
Duke St, Wisbech, Cambs PE13 2AE

NES-Arnold
Ludlow Hill Rd, W Bridgford, Nottingham NG2 6HD

# References

Burton, L. (1981) *Do You Panic About Maths?* Heinneman: Oxford.

Coupe, J. and Goldbart, J. (1988) *Communication before Speech,* Croom Helm: London.

DfEE (1998) *Supporting the Target Setting Process - Guidance for effective target setting for pupils with special educational needs,* HMSO: London.

DfEE/QCA (1999) *The Review of the National Curriculum in England - The Consultation Materials,* HMSO: London.

DfEE (1999) *The National Numeracy Strategy,* HMSO: London.

Dibb, D. (1990) *Internal Maths Trails* in Primary File 10, Mary Glasgow Publications: Glasgow.

Equals (1997) *Access to the whole curriculum for pupils with learning difficulties - Mathematics,* Equals: University of Northumbria at Newcastle.

Manchester Teacher Fellows - Banes, D. (ed) (1993) *Maths for All (2nd edition),* David Fulton: London.

McConkey, R. and McEvoy, J. (1986) *Count Me In: Videocourse on Nurturing Children's Counting and Number Skills,* St Michael's House: Dublin.

Merttens, R. and Vass, J. (1987) *Parents in schools: Raising money or Raising Standards,* Education 3-13 June 1987.

NCC (1991) *Curriculum Guidance 9: The National Curriculum and pupils with severe learning difficulties,* HMSO: London.

Ouvry, C. (1990) *Educating Children with Profound Handicaps,* BIMH Publications: Kidderminster.

Rhydderch-Evans, Z. (1995) *Mathematics in the School Grounds,* Southgate: London.

Rose, Sebba and Byers (1993) *Redefining the Curriculum for Pupils with Severe Learning Difficulties,* David Fulton: London.

SCAA (1996) *Desirable Outcomes for Children's Learning on Entering Compulsory Education,* HMSO: London.

Smith, B. (1987) *Interactive Approaches to the Education of Children With Severe Learning Difficulties,* Westhill College: Birmingham.

# Computer Software

**Writing with Symbols - Widgit Software**
102 Radford Rd, Leamington Spa, Warks. CV31 1LF

**Clicker - Crick Computing**
35 Charter Gate, Quarry Park Close, Moulton Park, Northampton NN3 6QB

**Sherston Software**
Angel House, Sherston, Malmesbury, Wilts. SN16 OLH

**Longman Logotron**
124 Cambridge Science Park, Milton Road, Cambridge CB4 0ZS